S0-AEC-793

TABLE OF CONTENTS

The Catholic
Theological Union
LIBRARY
Chicago, Ill.
WITHDRAWN

THE ORPHIC HYMNS

SOCIETY OF BIBLICAL LITERATURE
TEXTS AND TRANSLATIONS
GRAECO-ROMAN RELIGION SERIES

edited by

Hans Dieter Betz

and

Edward N. O'Neil

Texts and Translations 12
Graeco-Roman Religion Series 4
THE ORPHIC HYMNS
by
Apostolos N. Athanassakis

SCHOLARS PRESS
Missoula, Montana

THE ORPHIC HYMNS
Text, Translation and Notes

by

Apostolos N. Athanassakis

The Catholic Theological Union LIBRARY Chicago, Ill.

Published by
SCHOLARS PRESS
for
The Society of Biblical Literature

Distributed by

SCHOLARS PRESS
University of Montana
Missoula, Montana 59812

THE ORPHIC HYMNS
by
Apostolos N. Athanassakis

Copyright © 1977

by

The Society of Biblical Literature

Library of Congress Cataloging in Publication Data

Orpheus. Hymni.
    The Orphic Hymns.

    (Graeco-Roman religion series ; 4) (Texts and
translations ; 12)
    Bibliography: p.
    1. Hymns, English — Translations from Greek.
2. Hymns, Greek — Translations into English.
3. Dionysia. I. Title. II. Series. III. Series:
Society of Biblical Literature. Texts and translations ;
12.
BL820.B2076 1977   292'.3'8   76-54179
ISBN 0-89130-119-4

Printed in the United States of America

INTRODUCTION

Antiquity is virtually silent on the *Orphic Hymns*. The oldest reference to them is found in a scholium on Hesiod's *Theogony* by Ioannes Galenos (first half of the 12th century A.D.). Galenos refers to them three times in the same scholium but says nothing about their authorship or literary value.

A date of composition cannot be assigned to the Hymns with any certainty. Scholarly opinion on the subject has vacillated chiefly within the first four centuries of our era, but some would want to take the date of composition as far back as the sixth century B.C., while their opponents would settle for a Byzantine date. Neither of the two last extremes is now taken seriously. A few ancient sources make direct or oblique references to Orphic hymns, but they need not refer to our *Orphic Hymns*. It is much more reasonable to assume that the expression "Hymns of Orpheus" (cf. Plato *Laws* 829D-E; Pausanias 9.30.12) does not refer to a specific collection such as the one at our disposal but rather to Orphic poetry - perhaps even of the oral variety - which was attributed to the founder of Orphism. In the first oration against Aristogeiton (XI/772) Demosthenes tells us, "Orpheus says that she (sc. Dike) sits beside the throne of Zeus and watches over all human matters." The similarity between this statement and lines 2-3 of *Orphic Hymn* 62 (To Dike) has been noticed, but it would be unwise to build a hypothesis of composition on what must have become a common metaphor (cf. Hesiod *Works and Days* 259; Sophocles *Oedipus Coloneus* 1382). Scant and vague as the references to "Hymns of Orpheus" are in ancient sources, they cannot be used as evidence for the surviving collection. But the Hymns may have existed quite early and gone unnoticed on account of their literary mediocrity. After all,

antiquity treated the much older and much more beautiful
Homeric Hymns with astonishing indifference. I tend to
think that those scholars who place the composition of
the Hymns within the first four centuries of our era are
probably closer to the truth. The relative purity of the
language and the nearly flawless hexameter would argue
for the earlier part of this period. So would also the
remarkable absence of anything faintly Christian. There
is syncretism, but the syncretism is that of unmistakably
pagan elements. It is true that we have no evidence for
the existence of Orphic cults either in the first century
A.D. or, much less, in the later Roman imperial period.
On the other hand, the predilection of the Severan dynas-
ty (193-235 A.D.) for eastern institutions and ideas
favored a movement for religious reform and tolerance
which eventually culminated into the resuscitation and
flourishing of many mystic, especially Dionysiac, cults.
It may have been exactly in this sort of climate and at
some such time that underground remnants of Orphism sur-
faced again to reassert the tenacity of the old Thracian
divine musician. Perhaps then a date in the second part
of the third century A.D. is as good a guess as any.

The place in which the Hymns were composed and used
is not known, but here again scholars have not resisted
the temptation of conjecture. The appearance in the
Hymns of divinities hardly known or totally unknown to
mainland Greece should shift our attention eastward to
Asia Minor where, in fact, the names of some of these less
known Asiatic gods have been consistently turning up in
inscriptions. The three most telling names are Mise,
Hipta and Melinoe, all three previously known only from
the Hymns until the soil of western Anatolia revealed
their existence in inscriptions. Otto Kern was the first
to suggest that Pergamum was the birthplace of the Hymns,
and that they were used in mystic Dionysiac ceremonies in
the *temenos* of Demeter in that city (see "Das Demeter-

heiligtum von Pergamon und die orphischen Hymnen" *Hermes*
46 (1911) 431-36). His suggestion has found both sympa-
thizers and critics among scholars. Until epigraphic and
other evidence points to some other place we might consider Kern's theory a distinct possibility.

There is little to force us to the assumption of a
single authorship for all the Hymns. They do give the
impression of being the work of a religious antiquary who
had ready access to some sort of concordance from which
he marshaled forth hosts of epithets which he then linked
together as hexameters. This was more or less the view
of Lobeck, a view which is bound to be shared by those
who view the Hymns as literature rather than merely as
religious documents. Dieterich and Kern, and more re-
cently W.K.C. Guthrie have taken exception to this opinion. It is reasonable to think that when in the third
century many Dionysiac cults were revived and made to
serve as a convenient umbrella for the resuscitation of
Orphic elements, revered literary sources were tapped for
the creation of appropriate cult literature. And it is
equally reasonable to assume that newly founded θίασοι,
or cult associations, commissioned one or more able men
to provide them with religious poetry which should be as
authentic and comprehensive as possible.

It seems quite clear that the Hymns were used by a
religious association (θίασος) of people who called themselves μύσται, μυστιπόλοι, ὀργιοφάνται (mystic initiates)
and who, through prayer (εὐχή), libation (λοιβή), sacrifice (θυσία) and, presumably, secret ceremonies (ὄργια,
τελεταί) invoked a deity and asked for its presence or
for the gift of some blessing, such as wealth, peace,
health, and not infrequently for "a blameless end to a
good life." It is quite natural to assume that such a
θίασος would have its officers, and that the so called
βουκόλος, 'oxherd,' (mentioned in 1.10 and 31.7) was a

hierarch invested with sacerdotal power. The most pervasive characteristic of the Hymns, the ubiquitous epithet, might betoken a link between these Hymns and the various remains of magic literature from the Hellenistic and Roman periods. The idea seems to be that a propitiatory address to the deity, accompanied by as comprehensive a list of its powers and properties as possible, will force it to accede to one's wishes.

Most of the Hymns are addressed to divinities and concepts of the Hellenic pantheon and its train of lesser divine or semi-divine figures. Although a glance at the sequence of titles reveals some attempt at classification, the order of the Hymns does not follow any genealogical or hierarchic system. Such hymns as those to Ether, Stars, Nature (Physis), Boreas, Zephyros, Notos, being personifications of natural phenomena, may point to Stoic influence. So may also the invocation of Pronoia (Providence) in the proemic piece (line 30). Such personified abstractions as Dike, Dikaiosyne, Nomos are so old and so common to various schools of Greek philosophical and religious thought as not to be especially Orphic. The only hymn to a god of near eastern origin is the one to Adonis. Three hymns are dedicated to Phrygian goddesses (Mise, Hipta, Melinoe). The Orphic sympathies of the collection are nowhere more evident than in the number and fervor of individual pieces addressed to Dionysos. There are seven such hymns, while Zeus has only three that are specifically addressed to him. Dionysos is also frequently invoked or alluded to in many other hymns, and his characteristic epithets seem to have been so infectious or to have assumed such universal significance as to seriously have encroached upon the territory of other deities. This is as it should be, since Dionysos eventually became the chief Orphic god, and since it was a revival of his cult that created a favorable climate for a concomitant revival of Orphism.

Bits and pieces of Orphism are evident throughout the collection. There is no hint anywhere of animal sacrifices and of meat-eating, even if Dionysos himself is addressed as ὠμάδιος (i.e. 'taker of raw flesh'). This we may interpret as a concession to the non-Orphic side of the god and as part of the comprehensiveness of poems which are essentially conjuring formulae. Interestingly enough, it seems to be the persistent Orphic aversion to the crime of ὠμοφαγία (eating of raw flesh and consequently the dismemberment of Dionysos) that accounts for its suppression in the hymn to the Titans (37). It will be remembered by the reader that the Titans had dismembered and eaten Dionysos, and that Zeus destroyed them with the fire of his thunderbolt. Also Orphic, but not uniquely Orphic, is the sentiment expressed in the variations of the concluding formula "grant a good end to a life of industry, etc.," since a good life on earth attended by the proper rites of initiation and purification constitutes some sort of guarantee of rewards or, at least, of escape from punishment in the afterlife. To the Orphics the body was a prison for the soul, and the sentiment expressed in lines 1-5 of the very last hymn (87), referring as it does to a very central and basic belief, serves as an unmistakably Orphic capstone of an edifice to which other religions and philosophical systems made generous contributions.

Despite occasional hints, there is little or nothing in these hymns about Orphic theogony, anthropogony, or eschatology. To be sure Protogonos is equated with Phanes and is addressed as "born of an egg, delighting in his golden wings" (6.2). Orphic anthropogony is alluded to in the hymn to the Titans:

From you stem all toiling mortals,
the creatures of the sea and of the land, the birds,
and all generations of this world come from you.
(37.4-6)

Kronos and Chronos are characteristically equated in 13.5 where Kronos is called "begetter of time." And certainly the phrase "dreadful Necessity governs all" (3.11) must have been pregnant with meaning for the Orphic, since Ananke (Necessity) mated with Chronos (Time) to give birth to Ether, Chaos, and Erebos (Primeval Darkness). She was also consort of the Demiourgos (Creator) and mother of Heimarmene (Fate). But apropos of Ananke (for which see *Orphicorum Fragmenta* 54), it should be said that it is a concept which is found in the Presocratics, Plato, the tragedians, the Pythagoreans, and even in the cults of Mithras and Hermes Trismegistos, not to mention the Neoplatonists and the Neopythagoreans.

All this brings us to a very important and very frustrating question. Can we be certain about the specific relationship of the Hymns to various schools of philosophy? The hymn to Physis (10) could be claimed by Stoics, Neoplatonists, and even Neopythagoreans. The hymn to Apollon (34) has a definite Neopythagorean flavor. Lines 3-4 in *Orpheus to Mousaios*, 5.4-5, 11.3 and 11.16-17, 19.1, and 66.9 all contain references to the fiery element and all may reflect Stoic belief. There is so much fusion of different philosophical ideas in these hymns that the only thing that can be said of them in this regard is that they represent a confluence and a monument to the syncretism which characterized religion of the late Roman empire. Their composer or composers were not interested in creating a religious or philosophical system. The initiates wanted to protect their lives and save their souls. And to this end they needed the good will of every god and demon. The texts which they used in their rites are interesting not so much as poetry but rather as repositories of religious ideas, frequently borrowed from older literature and expressed by means peculiar to a category of the hymnic genre. It is a careful linguistic study of the provenience of many of the epithets in the hymns - especially the *hapax legomena* - that may help us answer some of the vexing questions that surround them.

The first manuscript of the Hymns to reach the west was the one carried to Venice by Giovanni Aurispa in 1423. It seems that another manuscript was taken to Italy by Franciscus Philelphus four years later (1427). Both of these manuscripts and perhaps four others have been lost. The loss of the manuscript brought to Venice by Aurispa is especially regrettable since it may have served as the archetype of all the surviving codices. Of these we have thirty-six, twenty-five on paper and eleven on skin. Some of these codices contain only a portion of the Hymns. The same codices frequently contain the *Homeric Hymns,* Hesiodea, the Orphic *Argonautica,* and the Hymns of Proklos and Kallimachos. As for the date of the codices, it seems safe to infer that they were all copied between 1450 and 1550.

We have reason to believe that the codex Aurispa brought with him from Constantinople in 1423 stirred up considerable excitement among the learned. On the other hand, it may not have been until the arrival in Venice of the Greek sage Georgios Gemistos (usually surnamed Plethon) some time in the middle of the fifteenth century that the Italians really took notice of the *Orphic Hymns.* The editio princeps was printed in Florence in 1500. It also contains the Orphic *Argonautica* and some of the Hymns of Proklos. By the year 1600 there were five more editions, one of which was the Aldine in 1517. From the editions which followed in subsequent centuries the one that excels all others - perhaps to this day - is Gottfried Hermann's (*Orphica, cum notis H. Stephani A. Chr. Eschenbachii I.M. Gesneri Th. Tyrwhitti,* Leipzig 1805). Abel's edition in 1885 has been received with adverse criticism. Wilhelm Quandt had finished his edition by 1941, but the vicissitudes of the war forced most scholars to wait until 1955 to reap the benefits of his

xiii

labors from its reprinted and somewhat augmented version.

The text used for this translation is that by Wilhelm Quandt (*Weidmannsche Verlagsbuchhandlung*), and the publishers deserve gratitude for granting us permission to use this text. The Orphic Hymns present the translator with an almost impossible task. The subject matter is complex and obscure, and some of the compound epithets require whole sentences for rendition into English. Professors Hans Dieter Betz and Edward N. O'Neil, editors of the series, are thanked for their insightful suggestions and careful scrutiny of introduction, translation, and notes. For help with proofreading credit is given to Mr. Walter Englert (M.A. Classics). And as sole reward for his labors the translator begs to dedicate this work to his colleague and friend, Birger A. Pearson, as μεγίστης φιλίας τεκμήριον ἐλάχιστον.

Apostolos N. Athanassakis
Santa Barbara, California
June, 1976

ΟΡΦΕΥΣ ΠΡΟΣ ΜΟΥΣΑΙΟΝ.

Εὐτυχῶς χρῶ, ἑταῖρε.

Μάνθανε δή, Μουσαῖε, θυηπολίην περισέμνην,
εὐχήν, ἣ δή τοι προφερεστέρη ἐστὶν ἀπασέων.
Ζεῦ βασιλεῦ καὶ Γαῖα καὶ οὐράνιαι φλόγες ἁγναὶ
Ἠελίου, Μήνης θ᾽ ἱερὸν σέλας Ἄστρα τε πάντα·
καὶ σύ, Ποσείδαον γαιήοχε, κυανοχαῖτα,   5
Φερσεφόνη θ᾽ ἁγνὴ Δημήτηρ τ᾽ ἀγλαόκαρπε
Ἄρτεμί ⟨τ᾽⟩ ἰοχέαιρα, κόρη, καὶ ἦιε Φοῖβε,
ὃς Δελφῶν ναίεις ἱερὸν πέδον· ὅς τε μεγίστας
τιμὰς ἐν μακάρεσσιν ἔχεις, Διόνυσε χορευτά·
Ἄρές τ᾽ ὀμβριμόθυμε καὶ Ἡφαίστου μένος ἁγνὸν   10
ἀφρογενής τε θεά, μεγαλώνυμα δῶρα λαχοῦσα·
καὶ σύ, καταχθονίων βασιλεῦ, μέγ᾽ ὑπείροχε δαῖμον,
Ἥβη τ᾽ Εἰλείθυια καὶ Ἡρακλέος μένος ἠΰ·
καὶ τὸ Δικαιοσύνης τε καὶ Εὐσεβίης μέγ᾽ ὄνειαρ
κικλήσκω Νύμφας τε κλυτὰς καὶ Πᾶνα μέγιστον   15
Ἥρην τ᾽, αἰγιόχοιο Διὸς θαλερὴν παράκοιτιν·
Μνημοσύνην τ᾽ ἐρατὴν Μούσας τ᾽ ἐπικέκλομαι ἁγνὰς
ἐννέα καὶ Χάριτάς τε καὶ Ὥρας ἠδ᾽ Ἐνιαυτὸν
Λητώ τ᾽ εὐπλόκαμον, Θείην σεμνήν τε Διώνην
Κουρῆτάς τ᾽ ἐνόπλους Κορύβαντάς τ᾽ ἠδὲ Καβείρους   20
καὶ μεγάλους Σωτῆρας ὁμοῦ, Διὸς ἄφθιτα τέκνα,
Ἰδαίους τε θεοὺς ἠδ᾽ ἄγγελον Οὐρανιώνων,
Ἑρμείαν κήρυκα, Θέμιν θ᾽, ἱεροσκόπον ἀνδρῶν,
Νύκτα τε πρεσβίστην καλέω καὶ φωσφόρον Ἧμαρ,

ORPHEUS TO MOUSAIOS
Friend, use it to good fortune.

Learn now, Mousaios, a rite mystic and most holy,
a prayer which surely excels all others.
Kind Zeus and Gaia, heavenly and pure flames
of the Sun, sacred light of the Moon, and all the
    Stars;
5   Poseidon, too, dark-maned holder of the earth,
pure Persephone and Demeter of the splendid fruit,
Artemis, the arrow-pouring maiden, and you kindly
    Phoibos
who dwell on the sacred ground of Delphoi. And
    Dionysos,
the dancer, whose honors among the blessed gods are
    the highest.
10   Strong-spirited Ares, holy and mighty Hephaistos,
and the goddess foam-born to whose lot fell
    sublime gifts,
and you, divinity excellent, who are king of the
    Underworld.
I call upon Hebe, and Eileithyia, and the noble
    ardor of Herakles,
the great blessings of justice and piety,
15   the glorious Nymphs and Pan the greatest,
and upon Hera, buxom wife of aegis-bearing Zeus.
I also call upon lovely Mnemosyne and the holy
    Muses,
all nine, as well as upon the Graces, the Seasons,
    the Year,
fair-tressed Leto, divine and revered Dione,
20   the armed Kouretes, the Korybantes, the Kabeiroi,
great Saviors, Zeus' ageless scions,
the Idaian gods, and upon Hermes, messenger and
    herald
of those in heaven; upon Themis, too, diviner of men
I call and on Night, oldest of all, and light-
    bringing Day;

4

25 Πίστιν τ᾽ ἠδὲ Δίκην καὶ ἀμύμονα Θεσμοδότειραν,
Ῥείαν τ᾽ ἠδὲ Κρόνον καὶ Τηθὺν κυανόπεπλον
Ὠκεανόν τε μέγαν, σύν τ᾽ Ὠκεανοῖο θύγατρας
Ἄτλαντός τε καὶ Αἰῶνος μέγ᾽ ὑπείροχον ἰσχὺν
καὶ Χρόνον ἀέναον καὶ τὸ Στυγὸς ἀγλαὸν ὕδωρ
30 μειλιχίους τε θεούς, ἀγαθήν τ᾽ ἐπὶ τοῖσι Πρόνοιαν
Δαίμονά τ᾽ ἠγάθεον καὶ Δαίμονα πήμονα θνητῶν,
Δαίμονας οὐρανίους καὶ ἠερίους καὶ ἐνύδρους
καὶ χθονίους καὶ ὑποχθονίους ἠδ᾽ ἐμπυριφοίτους,
καὶ Σεμέλην Βάκχου τε συνευαστῆρας ἅπαντας,
35 Ἰνὼ Λευκοθέην τε Παλαίμονά τ᾽ ὀλβιοδώτην
Νίκην θ᾽ ἡδυέπειαν ἰδ᾽ Ἀδρήστειαν ἄνασσαν
καὶ βασιλῆα μέγαν Ἀσκληπιὸν ἠπιοδώτην
Παλλάδα τ᾽ ἐγρεμάχην κούρην, Ἀνέμους τε πρόπαντας
καὶ Βροντὰς Κόσμου τε μέρη τετρακίονος αὐδῶ ·
40 Μητέρα τ᾽ ἀθανάτων, Ἄττιν καὶ Μῆνα κικλήσκω
Οὐρανίαν τε θεάν, σύν τ᾽ ἄμβροτον ἁγνὸν Ἄδωνιν
Ἀρχήν τ᾽ ἠδὲ Πέρας — τὸ γὰρ ἔπλετο πᾶσι μέγιστον —
εὐμενέας ἐλθεῖν κεχαρημένον ἦτορ ἔχοντας
τήνδε θυηπολίην ἱερὴν σπονδήν τ᾽ ἐπὶ σεμνήν.

1 ⟨Ἑκάτης⟩.

Εἰνοδίαν Ἑκάτην κλήιζω, τριοδῖτιν, ἐραννήν,
οὐρανίαν χθονίαν τε καὶ εἰναλίαν, κροκόπεπλον,
τυμβιδίαν, ψυχαῖς νεκύων μέτα βακχεύουσαν,
Περσείαν, φιλέρημον, ἀγαλλομένην ἐλάφοισι,
5 νυκτερίαν, σκυλακῖτιν, ἀμαιμάκετον βασίλειαν,
θηρόβρομον, ἄζωστον, ἀπρόσμαχον εἶδος ἔχουσαν,

25 then upon Faith, Dike, blameless Thesmodoteira,
   Rhea, Kronos, dark-veiled Tethys,
   the great Okeanos together with his daughters,
   the might preeminent of Atlas and Aion,
   Chronos the ever-flowing, the splendid water of
        the Styx,
30 all these gentle gods, and also Pronoia,
   and the holy Daimon as well as the one baneful to
        mortals;
   then upon divinities dwelling in heaven, air, water,
   on earth, under the earth, and in the fiery element.
35 Ino, Leukothee, Palaimon giver of bliss,
   sweet-speaking Nike, queenly Adresteia,
   the great king Asklepios who grants soothing,
   the battle-stirring maiden Pallas, all the Winds,
   Thunder, and the parts of the four-pillared Cosmos.
40 And I invoke the Mother of the immortals, Attis
        and Men,
   and the goddess Ouranie, immortal and holy Adonis,
   Beginning and End, too, which to all is most
        important,
   and ask them to come in a spirit of joyous mercy
   to this holy rite and libation of reverence.

                    1. TO HECATE

   Lovely Hekate of the roads and crossroads I invoke;
   in heaven, on earth, and in the sea, saffron-
        cloaked,
   tomb spirit reveling in the souls of the dead,
   daughter of Perses, haunting deserted places,
        delighting in deer,
5 nocturnal, dog-loving, monstrous queen,
   devouring wild beasts, ungirt, of repelling
        countenance.

ταυροπόλον, παντὸς κόσμου κληιδοῦχον ἄνασσαν,
ἡγεμόνην, νύμφην, κουροτρόφον, οὐρεσιφοῖτιν,
λισσόμενος κούρην τελεταῖς ὁσίαισι παρεῖναι
10 βουκόλωι εὐμενέουσαν ἀεὶ κεχαρηότι θυμῶι.

2 Προθυραίας, θυμίαμα στύρακα.

Κλῦθί μοι, ὦ πολύσεμνε θεά, πολυώνυμε δαῖμον,
ὠδίνων ἐπαρωγέ, λεχῶν ἡδεῖα πρόσοψι,
θηλειῶν σώτειρα μόνη, φιλόπαις, ἀγανόφρον,
ὠκυλόχεια, παροῦσα νέαις θνητῶν, Προθυραία,
5 κλειδοῦχ᾽, εὐάντητε, φιλοτρόφε, πᾶσι προσηνής,
ἣ κατέχεις οἴκους πάντων θαλίαις τε γέγηθας,
λυσίζων᾽, ἀφανής, ἔργοισι δὲ φαίνηι ἅπασι,
συμπάσχεις ὠδῖσι καὶ εὐτοκίηισι γέγηθας,
Εἰλείθυια, λύουσα πόνους δειναῖς ἐν ἀνάγκαις·
10 μούνην γὰρ σὲ καλοῦσι λεχοὶ ψυχῆς ἀνάπαυμα·
ἐν γὰρ σοὶ τοκετῶν λυσιπήμονές εἰσιν ἀνῖαι,
Ἄρτεμις Εἰλείθυια, † καὶ ἡ † σεμνή, Προθυραία.
κλῦθι, μάκαιρα, δίδου δὲ γονὰς ἐπαρωγὸς ἐοῦσα
καὶ σῶζ᾽, ὥσπερ ἔφυς αἰεὶ σώτειρα προπάντων.

3 Νυκτός, θυμίαμα δαλούς.

Νύκτα θεῶν γενέτειραν ἀείσομαι ἠδὲ καὶ ἀνδρῶν.
{Νὺξ γένεσις πάντων, ἣν καὶ Κύπριν καλέσωμεν}

You, herder of bulls, queen and mistress of the
    whole world,
leader, nymph, mountain-roaming nurturer of youth,
maiden, I beseech to come to these holy rites,
10   ever with joyous heart and ever favoring the oxherd.

2. TO PROTHYRAIA,
incense - storax

Hear me, revered goddess, many-named divinity.
You aid in travail, O sight sweet to women in labor;
you save women and *you* alone love children, O kindly
goddess of swift birth, ever helpful to young women,
    O **Prothyraia**.
5   Accessible to all, O mistress, you are gracious and
        fond of nurture,
yours is the power in every house and you delight
        in festivities;
you loosen girdles and, though invisible, you are
        seen in every deed.
You share pain, and rejoice in every birth,
O Eileithyia, freeing from pain those in terrible
    distress.
10   Upon you alone pregnant women call, O comforter of
        souls,
and in you alone there is relief from pains of
        labor.
Artemis, Eileithyia, reverend Prothyraia!
Hearken, O blessed one, succor me, grant offspring,
and save me, for it is your nature to be savior
    of all.

3. TO NIGHT,
incense - firebrands

I shall sing of Night, mother of gods and men.
(Night - and let us call her Kypris - gave birth
    to all.)

κλῦθι, μάκαιρα θεά, κυαναυγής, ἀστεροφεγγής,
ἡσυχίηι χαίρουσα καὶ ἠρεμίηι πολυύπνωι,
5 εὐφροσύνη, τερπνή, φιλοπάννυχε, μῆτερ ὀνείρων,
ληθομέριμν᾽ ἀγανή τε, πόνων ἀνάπαυσιν ἔχουσα,
ὑπνοδότειρα, φίλη πάντων, ἐλάσιππε, νυχαυγής,
ἡμιτελής, χθονία ἠδ᾽ οὐρανία πάλιν αὐτή,
ἐγκυκλία, παίκτειρα διώγμασιν ἠεροφοίτοις,
10 ἢ φάος ἐκπέμπεις ὑπὸ νέρτερα καὶ πάλι φεύγεις
εἰς Ἀίδην· δεινὴ γὰρ ἀνάγκη πάντα κρατύνει.
νῦν σε, μάκαιρα, ⟨καλ⟩ῶ, πολυόλβιε, πᾶσι ποθεινή,
εὐάντητε, κλύουσα ἱκετηρίδα φωνὴν
ἔλθοις εὐμενέουσα, φόβους δ᾽ ἀπόπεμπε νυχαυγεῖς.

4 Οὐρανοῦ, θυμίαμα λίβανον.

Οὐρανὲ παγγενέτωρ, κόσμου μέρος αἰὲν ἀτειρές,
πρεσβυγένεθλ᾽, ἀρχὴ πάντων πάντων τε τελευτή,
κόσμε πατήρ, σφαιρηδὸν ἑλισσόμενος περὶ γαῖαν,
οἶκε θεῶν μακάρων, ῥόμβου δίναισιν ὁδεύων,
5 οὐράνιος χθόνιός τε φύλαξ πάντων περιβληθείς,
ἐν στέρνοισιν ἔχων φύσεως ἄτλητον ἀνάγκην,
κυανόχρως, ἀδάμαστε, παναίολε, αἰολόμορφε,
πανδερκές, Κρονότεκνε, μάκαρ, πανυπέρτατε δαῖμον,
κλῦθ᾽ ἐπάγων .ζωὴν ὁσίαν μύστηι νεοφάντηι.

Hearken, O blessed goddess, jet-black and star-lit,
whose delight is in quiet and slumber-filled
   serenity.
5   Cheerful and delightsome, O mother of dreams, you
   love the nightlong revel,
and your gentleness rids of cares, and offers
   respite from toil.
Giver of sleep, beloved of all you are as you drive
   your steeds and gleam in darkness.
Ever incomplete, now terrestrial and now again
   celestial,
you circle around in pursuit of sprightly phantoms,
10   you force light into the nether world, and again
   you flee
into Hades. Dreadful Necessity governs all things.
But now, O blessed one - yea beatific and desired
   by all - I call on you
to grant a kind ear to my voice of supplication
and, benevolent, come to disperse fears that glisten
   in the night.

4. TO OURANOS,
incense - frankincense

Ouranos, father of all, eternal cosmic element,
primeval, beginning of all and end of all,
lord of the universe, moving about the earth like
   a sphere,
home of the blessed gods. Your motion is a roaring
   whirl,
5   and you envelop all as their celestial and terrestrial guard.
In your breast lies nature's invincible drive;
dark-blue, indomitable, shimmering, variform,
all-seeing father of Kronos, blessed and most
   sublime divinity,
hearken and bring a life of holiness to the newly
   initiated.

5 Αἰθέρος, θυμίαμα κρόκον.

Ὦ Διὸς ὑψιμέλαθρον ἔχων κράτος αἰὲν ἀτειρές,
ἄστρων ἠελίου τε σεληναίης τε μέρισμα,
πανδαμάτωρ, πυρίπνου, πᾶσι ζωοῖσιν ἔναυσμα,
ὑψιφανὴς Αἰθήρ, κόσμου στοιχεῖον ἄριστον,
5   ἀγλαὸν ὦ βλάστημα, σελασφόρον, ἀστεροφεγγές,
κικλήσκων λίτομαί σε κεκραμένον εὔδιον εἶναι.

6 Πρωτογόνου, θυμίαμα σμύρναν.

Πρωτόγονον καλέω διφυῆ, μέγαν, αἰθερόπλαγκτον,
ὠιογενῆ, χρυσέαισιν ἀγαλλόμενον πτερύγεσσι,
ταυροβόαν, γένεσιν μακάρων θνητῶν τ᾽ ἀνθρώπων,
σπέρμα πολύμνηστον, πολυόργιον, Ἡρικεπαῖον,
5   ἄρρητον, κρύφιον ῥοιζήτορα, παμφαὲς ἔρνος,
ὄσσων ὃς σκοτόεσσαν ἀπημαύρωσας ὀμίχλην
πάντη δινηθεὶς πτερύγων ῥιπαῖς κατὰ κόσμον
λαμπρὸν ἄγων φάος ἁγνόν, ἀφ᾽ οὗ σε Φάνητα κικλήσκω
ἠδὲ Πρίηπον ἄνακτα καὶ Ἀνταύγην ἑλίκωπον.
10   ἀλλά, μάκαρ, πολύμητι, πολύσπορε, βαῖνε γεγηθὼς
ἐς τελετὴν ἁγίαν πολυποίκιλον ὀργιοφάνταις.

5. TO ETHER,
incense - crocus

Yours are Zeus' lofty dwelling and endless power,
and of the stars, the sun, and the moon you claim
    a share.
O tamer of all, fire-breather, life's spark for
    every creature,
sublime Ether, best cosmic element,
5   radiant, luminous, starlit offspring,
I call upon you and beseech you to be temperate
    and clear.

6. TO PROTOGONOS,
incense - myrrh

Upon two-natured, great and ether-tossed Protogonos
    I call;
born of the egg, delighting in his golden wings,
he bellows like a bull, this begetter of blessed
    gods and mortal men.
Erikepaios, seed unforgettable, attended by many
    rites,
5   ineffable, hidden, brilliant scion, whose motion is
    whirring,
you scattered the dark mist that lay before your
    eyes
and, flapping your wings, you whirled about, and
    throughout this world
you brought pure light. For this I call you Phanes
and Lord Priapos and bright-eyed Antauges.
10   But O blessed one of the many counsels and seeds,
    come gladly
to the celebrants of this holy and elaborate rite.

7 Ἄστρων, θυμίαμα ἀρώματα.

Ἄστρων οὐρανίων ἱερὸν σέλας ἐκπροκαλοῦμαι
εὐιέροις φωναῖσι κικλήσκων δαίμονας ἁγ[ν]ούς.
Ἀστέρες οὐράνιοι, Νυκτὸς φίλα τέκνα μελαίνης,
ἐγκυκλίοις δίναισι † περιθρόνια κυκλέοντες.
5   ἀνταυγεῖς, πυρόεντες, ἀεὶ γενετῆρες ἁπάντων,
μοιρίδιοι, πάσης μοίρης σημάντορες ὄντες,
θνητῶν ἀνθρώπων θείαν διέποντες ἀταρπόν,
ἑπταφαεῖς ζώνας ἐφορώμενοι, ἠερόπλαγκτοι,
οὐράνιοι χθόνιοί τε, πυρίδρομοι, αἰὲν ἀτειρεῖς,
10   αὐγάζοντες ἀεὶ νυκτὸς ζοφοειδέα πέπλον,
μαρμαρυγαῖς στίλβοντες, ἐύφρονες ἐννύχιοί τε·
ἔλθετ᾽ ἐπ᾽ εὐιέρου τελετῆς πολυΐστορας ἄθλους
ἐσθλὸν ἐπ᾽ εὐδόξοις ἔργοις δρόμον ἐκτελέοντες.

8 Εἰς Ἥλιον, θυμίαμα λιβανομάνναν.

Κλῦθι μάκαρ, πανδερκὲς ἔχων αἰώνιον ὄμμα,
Τιτὰν χρυσαυγής, Ὑπερίων, οὐράνιον φῶς,
αὐτοφυής, ἀκάμα⟨ς⟩, ζώιων ἡδεῖα πρόσοψι,
δεξιὲ μὲν γενέτωρ ἠοῦς, εὐώνυμε νυκτός,
5   κρᾶσιν ἔχων ὡρῶν, τετραβάμοσι ποσσὶ χορεύων,
εὔδρομε, ῥιζωτήρ, πυρόεις, φαιδρωπέ, διφρευτά,
ῥόμβου ἀπειρεσίου δινεύμασιν οἶμον ἐλαύνων,
εὐσεβέσιν καθοδηγὲ καλῶν, ζαμενὴς ἀσεβοῦσι,
χρυσολύρη, κόσμου τὸν ἐναρμόνιον δρόμον ἔλκων,

7. TO THE STARS,
incense - aromatic herbs

I call forth the sacred light of the heavenly stars
and with devotional prayers I summon the holy
    demons.
Heavenly stars, dear children of dark Night,
on circles you march and whirl about,
5   O brilliant and fiery begetters of all.
Fate, everyone's fate you reveal,
and you determine the divine path for mortals
as, wandering in midair, you gaze upon the seven
    luminous orbits.
In heaven and on earth, ever indestructible on your
    blazing trail,
10   you shine upon night's cloak of darkness.
Coruscating, gleaming, kindly and nocturnal,
visit the learned contests of this sacred rite,
finishing a noble race for works of glory.

8. TO THE SUN,
incense - pounded frankincense

Hearken, O blessed one, whose eternal eye sees all,
Titan radiant as gold, Hyperion, celestial light,
self-born, untiring, sweet sight to living
    creatures,
on the right you beget dawn and on the left night.
5   You temper the seasons as you ride your dancing
    horses,
and rushing swiftly, O fiery and bright-faced
    charioteer,
you press on your course in endless whirl
and, harsh to the impious, you teach good to the
    pious.
Yours the golden lyre and the harmony of cosmic
    motion,

ἔργων σημάντωρ ἀγαθῶν, ὡροτρόφε κοῦρε,
κοσμοκράτωρ, συρικτά, πυρίδρομε, κυκλοέλικτε,
φωσφόρε, † αἰολόδικτε, φερέσβιε, κάρπιμε Παιάν,
ἀιθαλής, ἀμίαντε, χρόνου πάτερ, ἀθάνατε Ζεῦ,
εὔδιε, πασιφαής, κόσμου τὸ περίδρομον ὄμμα,
σβεννύμενε λάμπων τε καλαῖς ἀκτῖσι φαειναῖς,
δεῖκτα δικαιοσύνης, φιλονάματε, δέσποτα κόσμου,
πιστοφύλαξ, αἰεὶ πανυπέρτατε, πᾶσιν ἀρωγέ,
ὄμμα δικαιοσύνης, ζωῆς φῶς· ὦ ἐλάσιππε,
μάστιγι λιγυρῆι τετράορον ἅρμα διώκων·
κλῦθι λόγων, ἡδὺν δὲ βίον μύστηισι πρόφαινε.

9 Εἰς Σελήνην, θυμίαμα ἀρώματα.

Κλῦθι, θεὰ βασίλεια, φαεσφόρε, δῖα Σελήνη,
ταυρόκερως Μήνη, νυκτιδρόμε, ἠεροφοῖτι,
ἐννυχία, δαιδοῦχε, κόρη, εὐάστερε, † Μήνη,
αὐξομένη καὶ λειπομένη, θῆλύς τε καὶ ἄρσην,
αὐγάστειρα, φίλιππε, χρόνου μῆτερ, φερέκαρπε,
ἠλεκτρίς, βαρύθυμε, καταυγάστειρα, † νυχία,
πανδερκής, φιλάγρυπνε, καλοῖς ἄστροισι βρύουσα,
ἡσυχίηι χαίρουσα καὶ εὐφρόνηι ὀλβιομοίρωι,
λαμπετίη, χαριδῶτι, τελεσφόρε, νυκτὸς ἄγαλμα,

10   and you command noble deeds and nurture the seasons.
Piping lord of the world, a fiery circle of light
is your course, and, O Paian, your light gives life
        and fruit.
Eternal, pure, father of time, O immortal Zeus,
you are the clear, brilliant, and all-encompassing
        cosmic eye,
15   both when you set and when you shine your lovely
        and radiant light.
A paragon of justice, O water-loving lord of the
        cosmos,
you guard pledges and, ever the highest, you help
        all.
Eye of justice and light of life, O charioteer,
with screaming whip you drive the four-horsed
        chariot on.
20   Hear my words and show life's sweetness to the
        initiates.

                9.   TO THE MOON,
                        incense - aromatic herbs

Hearken, O divine queen, light-bringing and splendid
        Selene,
bull-horned Moon traversing the air in a race with
        night.
Nocturnal, torch-bearing, maiden of fair stars,
        Moon
waxing and waning, feminine and masculine,
5   glittering lover of horses, mother of time, bearer
        of fruit,
amber-colored, brooding, shining in the night,
all-seeing, vigilant, surrounded by beautiful stars,
you delight in quiet and in the richness of the
        night.
Shining in the night, like a jewel, you grant
        fulfillment and favor;

10 ἀστράρχη, τανύπεπλ᾽, ἑλικοδρόμε, πάνσοφε κούρη,
ἐλθέ, μάκαιρ᾽, εὔφρων, εὐάστερε, φέγγεϊ τρισσῶι
λαμπομένη, σώζουσα νέους ἱκέτας σέο, κούρη.

10 Φύσεως, θυμίαμα ἀρώματα.

Ὦ Φύσι, παμμήτειρα θεά, πολυμήχανε μῆτερ,
οὐρανία, πρέσβειρα, πολύκτιτε δαῖμον, ἄνασσα,
πανδαμάτωρ, ἀδάμαστε, κυβερνήτειρα, παναυγής,
παντοκράτειρα, † τιτιμενέα πανυπέρτατε πᾶσιν
5   ἄφθιτε, πρωτογένεια, παλαίφατε, κυδιάνειρα,
ἐννυχία, πολύπειρε, σελασφόρε, δεινοκάθεκτε,
ἄψοφον ἀστραγάλοισι ποδῶν ἴχνος εἱλίσσουσα,
ἁγνή, κοσμήτειρα θεῶν ἀτελής τε τελευτή,
κοινὴ μὲν πάντεσσιν, ἀκοινώνητε δὲ μούνη,
10   αὐτοπάτωρ, ἀπάτωρ, ἐρατή, † πολύγηθε, μεγίστη,
εὐάνθεια, πλοκή, φιλία, πολύμικτε, δαῆμον,
ἡγεμόνη, κράντειρα, φερέσβιε, παντρόφε κούρη,
αὐτάρκεια, δίκη, Χαρίτων πολυώνυμε πειθώ,
αἰθερία, χθονία καὶ εἰναλία μεδέουσα,
15   πικρὰ μὲν φαύλοισι, γλυκεῖα δὲ πειθομένοισι,
πάνσοφε, πανδώτειρα, κομίστρια, παμβασίλεια,
αὐξιτρόφος, πίειρα πεπαινομένων τε λύτειρα.
πάντων μὲν σὺ πατήρ, μήτηρ, τροφὸς ἠδὲ τιθηνός,
ὠκυλόχεια, μάκαιρα, πολύσπορος, ὡριὰς ὁρμή,

10   long-cloaked marshal of the stars, wise maiden whose
          motion is circular,
      come! Blessed and gentle lady of the stars, in
          three ways
      shine your redeeming light upon your new initiates.

                    10. TO PHYSIS,
                          incense - aromatic herbs

      O Physis, resourceful mother of all,
      celestial and rich divinity, oldest of all, queen,
      all-taming and indomitable, lustrous ruler,
      (ever honored) mistress of all, highest goddess,
5   imperishable, first-born, fabled glorifier of men,
      nocturnal, knowing, light-bringing, irrepressible.
      Swift is the motion of your feet and your steps
          noiseless,
      O pure marshal of the gods, end that has no end.
      All partake of you but you alone partake of no one;
10   self-fathered and hence fatherless; lovely, joyous,
          great,
      and accessible, you nurse flowers, you lovingly
          commingle and twine,
      and you lead, rule and bring life and nourishment
          to all.
      Self-sufficient, many-named persuasion of the
          Graces, Dike herself,
      queen of heaven and earth and sea,
15   you are bitter to the vulgar and sweet to those
          who obey you.
      Wise in all, giver of all, nurturing queen of all,
      abundant nourishment is yours, as you dissolve
          whatever ripens.
      Father and mother of all, nurturer and nurse,
      you bring swift birth, O blessed one, and a wealth
          of seeds and the fever of seasons are yours.

παντοτεχνές, πλάστειρα, πολύκτιτε, † ποντία δαῖμον,
ἀϊδία, κινησιφόρε, πολύπειρε, περίφρων,
ἀενάωι στροφάλιγγι θοὸν ῥύμα δινεύουσα,
πάνρυτε, κυκλοτερής, ἀλλοτριομορφοδίαιτε,
εὔθρονε, τιμήεσσα, μόνη τὸ κριθὲν τελέουσα,
σκηπτούχων ἐφύπερθε βαρυβρεμέτειρα κρατίστη,
ἄτρομε, πανδαμάτειρα, πεπρωμένη, αἶσα, πυρίπνους,
ἀίδιος Ζωὴ ἠδ᾽ ἀθανάτη τε πρόνοια·
πάντα † σοι εἰσὶ τὰ πάντα· † σὺ γὰρ μούνη τάδε τεύχεις.
ἀλλά, θεά, λίτομαί σε † σὺν εὐόλβοισιν † ἐν ὥραις
εἰρήνην ὑγίειαν ἄγειν, αὔξησιν ἁπάντων.

11 Πανός, θυμίαμα ποικίλα.

Πᾶνα καλῶ κρατερόν, νόμιον, κόσμοιο τὸ σύμπαν,
οὐρανὸν ἠδὲ θάλασσαν ἰδὲ χθόνα παμβασίλειαν
καὶ πῦρ ἀθάνατον· τάδε γὰρ μέλη ἐστὶ τὰ Πανός.
ἐλθέ, μάκαρ, σκιρτητά, περίδρομε, σύνθρονε Ὥραις,
αἰγομελές, βακχευτά, φιλένθεε, ἀστροδίαιτε,
ἁρμονίαν κόσμοιο κρέκων φιλοπαίγμονι μολπῇι,
φαντασιῶν ἐπαρωγέ, φόβων ἔκπαγλε βροτείων,
αἰγονόμοις χαίρων ἀνὰ πίδακας ἠδέ τε βούταις,
εὔσκοπε, θηρητήρ, Ἠχοῦς φίλε, σύγχορε νυμφῶν,

20   An opulent and mighty divinity, you give shape and
      form to all things;
  eternal, setting all in motion, skilled and
      discreet,
  you are ever turning the swift stream into an
      unceasing eddy.
  Flowing in all things, circular, ever changing form,
  fair-throned, precious, you alone accomplish your
      designs
25   and, loud-roaring, you rule mightily over sceptered
      kings.
  Fearless, all-taming, destined fate, fire-breathing,
  you are life everlasting and immortal providence.
  Since you fashion these things (you are everything).
  You are the all, for you alone do these things
30   to bring peace, health, and growth to all.

11. TO PAN,
incense - et varia

  I call upon Pan, the pastoral god, and upon the
      universe,
  that is, upon sky and sea and land, queen of all,
  and upon the immortal fire; all these are Pan's
      realm.
  Come, O blessed, frolicsome and restless companion
      of the seasons!
5   Goat-limbed, reveling, lover of frenzy, star-
      haunting,
  you weave your playful song into cosmic harmony,
  and you induce phantasies of dread into the minds
      of mortals.
  Your delight is at Springs, among goatherds and
      oxherds,
  and you dance with the nymphs, you keen-eyed hunter
      and lover of Echo.

10 παντοφυής, γενέτωρ πάντων, πολυώνυμε δαῖμον,
κοσμοκράτωρ, αὐξητά, φαεσφόρε, κάρπιμε Παιάν,
ἀντροχαρές, βαρύμηνις, ἀληθὴς Ζεὺς ὁ κεράστης.
σοὶ γὰρ ἀπειρέσιον γαίης πέδον ἐστήρικται,
εἴκει δ' ἀκαμάτου πόντου τὸ βαθύρροον ὕδωρ
15 Ὠκεανός τε πέριξ † ἐν ὕδασι † γαῖαν ἑλίσσων,
ἀέριόν τε μέρισμα τροφῆς, ζωοῖσιν ἔναυσμα,
καὶ κορυφῆς ἐφύπερθεν ἐλαφροτάτου πυρὸς ὄμμα.
βαίνει γὰρ τάδε θεῖα πολύκριτα σαῖσιν ἐφετμαῖς·
ἀλλάσσεις δὲ φύσεις πάντων ταῖς σαῖσι προνοίαις
20 βόσκων ἀνθρώπων γενεὴν κατ' ἀπείρονα κόσμον.
ἀλλά, μάκαρ, βακχευτά, φιλένθεε, βαῖν' ἐπὶ λοιβαῖς
εὐιέροις, ἀγαθὴν δ' ὄπασον βιότοιο τελευτὴν
Πανικὸν ἐκπέμπων οἶστρον ἐπὶ τέρματα γαίης.

12 Ἡρακλέος, θυμίαμα λίβανον.

Ἡράκλες ὀμβριμόθυμε, μεγασθενές, ἄλκιμε Τιτάν,
καρτερόχειρ, ἀδάμαστε, βρύων ἄθλοισι κραταιοῖς,
αἰολόμορφε, χρόνου πάτερ, † ἀίδιέ τε † εὔφρων,
ἄρρητ', ἀγριόθυμε, πολύλλιτε, παντοδυνάστα,
5 παγκρατὲς ἦτορ ἔχων, κάρτος μέγα, τοξότα, μάντι,
παμφάγε, παγγενέτωρ, πανυπέρτατε, πᾶσιν ἀρωγέ,
ὃς θνητοῖς κατέπαυσας ἀνήμερα φῦλα διώξας,
εἰρήνην ποθέων κουροτρόφον, ἀγλαότιμ[ον],
αὐτοφυής, ἀκάμας, γαίης βλάστημα φέριστον,

10   Present in all growth, begetter of all, many-named
          divinity,
      lord of the cosmos, light-bringing and fructifying
          Paian,
      cave-loving and wrathful, a veritable Zeus with
          horns.
      The earth's endless plain is supported by you,
      and to you yield the deep-flowing water of the
          untiring sea,
15   and Okeanos who girds the earth with his eddying
          stream,
      and the air we breathe, which kindles all life,
      and, above us, the sublime eye of weightless fire.
      At your behest, all these are kept wide apart.
      Your providence alters the natures of all,
20   and on the boundless earth you offer nourishment to
          mankind.
      Come, frenzy-loving and gamboling god; come to
          these sacred
      libations, bring my life to a good conclusion,
      and send Pan's madness to the ends of the earth.

                    12.   TO HERAKLES,
                            incense - frankincense

      Herakles, stout-hearted and mighty, powerful Titan,
      strong-handed, indomitable, author of valiant deeds,
      you change your form, O everlasting and kindly
          father of time.
      Ineffable, wild, lord of all to whom many pray,
5   all-conquering and mettlesome, archer and seer,
      omnivorous begetter of all, and most sublime helper,
      who, for the sake of men, subdued and tamed savage
          races
      because you desired peace, which brings dazzling
          honors and nurtures youths.
      Self-grown, unwearying, bravest child of the earth.

10 πρωτογόνοις στράψας βολίσιν, μεγαλώνυμε Παιών,
ὃς περὶ κρατὶ φορεῖς ἠῶ καὶ νύκτα μέλαιναν,
δώδεκ' ἀπ' ἀντολιῶν ἄχρι δυσμῶν ἆθλα διέρπων,
ἀθάνατος, πολύπειρος, ἀπείριτος, ἀστυφέλικτος·
ἐλθέ, μάκαρ, νούσων θελκτήρια πάντα κομίζων,
15 ἐξέλασον δὲ κακὰς ἄτας κλάδον ἐν χερὶ πάλλων,
πτηνοῖς τ' ἰοβόλοις κῆρας χαλεπὰς ἀπόπεμπε.

13 Κρόνου, θυμίαμα στύρακα.

Ἀιθαλής, μακάρων τε θεῶν πάτερ ἠδὲ καὶ ἀνδρῶν,
ποικιλόβουλ', ἀμίαντε, μεγασθενές, ἄλκιμε Τιτάν,
ὃς δαπανᾷς μὲν ἅπαντα καὶ αὔξεις ἔμπαλιν αὐτός,
δεσμοὺς ἀρρήκτους ὃς ἔχεις κατ' ἀπείρονα κόσμον,
5 αἰῶνος Κρόνε παγγενέτωρ, Κρόνε ποικιλόμυθε,
Γαίης τε βλάστημα καὶ Οὐρανοῦ ἀστερόεντος,
γέννα, φυή, μείωσι, Ῥέας πόσι, σεμνὲ Προμηθεῦ,
ὃς ναίεις κατὰ πάντα μέρη κόσμοιο, γενάρχα,
ἀγκυλομῆτα, φέριστε· κλύων ἱκετηρίδα φωνὴν
10 πέμποις εὔολβον βιότου τέλος αἰὲν ἄμεμπτον.

14 Ῥέας, θυμίαμα ἀρώματα.

Πότνα Ῥέα, θύγατερ πολυμόρφου Πρωτογόνοιο,
ἥτ' ἐπὶ ταυροφόνων ἱερότροχον ἅρμα τιταίνεις,
τυμπανόδουπε, φιλοιστρομανές, χαλκόκροτε κούρη,
μῆτερ Ζηνὸς ἄνακτος Ὀλυμπίου, αἰγιόχοιο,

10 You hurled your primeval thunderbolts,
        O illustrious Paion
    Round your head dawn and dark night cling,
    and your twelve deeds of valor stretch from east to
        west.
    Immortal, world-wise, boundless and irrepressible,
    come, O blessed one, bringing all charms against
        disease;
15 with club in hand, drive evil bane away
    and with your poisonous darts ward off cruel death.

13. TO KRONOS,
incense - storax

Everlasting father of blessed gods and men,
resourceful, pure, mighty and powerful Titan,
you consume all things and replenish them, too.
Unbreakable is the hold you have on the boundless
    cosmos,
5   O Kronos, begetter of time, Kronos of contrasting
        discourse,
child of earth and starry sky.
In you there is birth and decline, august and pru-
    dent lord of Rhea,
who, as progenitor, dwell in every part of the
    world.
Hear my suppliant voice, O wily and brave one,
10 and bring an ever blameless end to a good life.

14. TO RHEA,
incense - aromatic herbs

Mighty Rhea, daughter of many-faced Protogonos,
your sacred chariot is drawn by bull-slaying lions.
The sound of drums and cymbals, O frenzy-loving
    maiden,
is yours, and you are the mother of the aegis-
    bearing Olympian lord.

πάντιμ', ἀγλαόμορφε, Κρόνου σύλλεκτρε μάκαιρα,
οὔρεσιν ἢ χαίρεις θνητῶν τ' ὀλολύγμασι φρικτοῖς,
παμβασίλεια 'Ρέα, πολεμόκλονε, ὀμβριμόθυμε,
ψευδομένη, σώτειρα, λυτηριάς, ἀρχιγένεθλε,
μήτηρ μέν τε θεῶν ἠδὲ θνητῶν ἀνθρώπων·
ἐκ σοῦ γὰρ καὶ γαῖα καὶ οὐρανὸς εὐρὺς ὕπερθεν
καὶ πόντος πνοιαί τε· φιλόδρομε, ἀερόμορφε·
ἐλθέ, μάκαιρα θεά, σωτήριος εὔφρονι βουλῆι
εἰρήνην κατάγουσα σὺν εὐόλβοις κτεάτεσσι,
λύματα καὶ κῆρας πέμπουσ' ἐπὶ τέρματα γαίης.

15 Διός, θυμίαμα στύρακα.

Ζεῦ πολυτίμητε, Ζεῦ ἄφθιτε, τήνδε τοι ἡμεῖς
μαρτυρίαν τιθέμεσθα λυτήριον ἠδὲ πρόσευξιν.
ὦ βασιλεῦ, διὰ σὴν κεφαλὴν ἐφάνη τάδε θεῖα,
γαῖα θεὰ μήτηρ ὀρέων θ' ὑψηχέες ὄχθοι
καὶ πόντος καὶ πάνθ', ὁπόσ' οὐρανὸς ἐντὸς ἔταξε·
Ζεῦ Κρόνιε, σκηπτοῦχε, καταιβάτα, ὀμβριμόθυμε,
παντογένεθλ', ἀρχὴ πάντων πάντων τε τελευτή,
σεισίχθων, αὐξητά, καθάρσιε, παντοτινάκτα,
ἀστραπαῖε, βρονταῖε, κεραύνιε, φυτάλιε Ζεῦ·
κλῦθί μου, αἰολόμορφε, δίδου δ' ὑγίειαν ἀμεμφῆ
εἰρήνην τε θεὰν καὶ πλούτου δόξαν ἄμεμπτον.

5   Illustrious and honored, you are Kronos' blessed
       consort
    and you delight in the mountains and in the horrid
       shrieks of mortals.
    Strong-spirited Rhea, queen of queens, lover of the
       battle din,
    liar, savior, redeemer, first by birth,
    you are mother of gods and mortal men.

10   From you come the earth, the wide sky above,
    the sea and the winds. Ethereal and restless,
    come, O blessed goddess, as gentle-minded savior,
    bring peace and a wealth of possessions,
    and send death and mire to the ends of the earth.

15. TO ZEUS,
incense - storax

Much-honored Zeus, indestructible Zeus, we lay
before you this redeeming testimony and this
    prayer:
O King, you have brought to light divine works,
and earth, goddess and mother, the hills swept by
    the shrill winds,

5   the sea, and the host of stars marshaled by the sky.
Kronian Zeus, whose sceptre is the thunderbolt,
    strong-spirited,
father of all, beginning and end of all,
earth-shaker, increaser and purifier; indeed, All-
    Shaker,
god of thunder and lightning, Zeus the planter.

10   Hear me, O many-faced one, and grant me unblemished
    health,
divine peace, and riches and glory without blame.

16 Ἥρης, θυμίαμα ἀρώματα.

Κυανέοις κόλποισιν ἐνημένη, ἀερόμορφε,
Ἥρα παμβασίλεια, Διὸς σύλλεκτρε μάκαιρα,
ψυχοτρόφους αὔρας θνητοῖς παρέχουσα προσηνεῖς,
ὄμβρων μὲν μήτηρ, ἀνέμων τροφέ, παντογένεθλε·
5   χωρὶς γὰρ σέθεν οὐδὲν ὅλως Ζωῆς φύσιν ἔγνω·
κοινωνεῖς γὰρ ἅπασι κεκραμένη ἠέρι σεμνῶι·
πάντων γὰρ κρατέεις μούνη πάντεσσί τ᾽ ἀνάσσεις
ἠερίοις ῥοίζοισι τινασσομένη κατὰ χεῦμα.
ἀλλά, μάκαιρα θεά, πολυώνυμε, παμβασίλεια,
10   ἔλθοις εὐμενέουσα καλῶι γήθουσα προσώπωι.

17 Ποσειδῶνος, θυμίαμα σμύρναν.

Κλῦθι, Ποσείδαον γαιήοχε, κυανοχαῖτα,
ἵππιε, χαλκοτόρευτον ἔχων χείρεσσι τρίαιναν,
ὃς ναίεις πόντοιο βαθυστέρνοιο θέμεθλα,
ποντομέδων, ἁλίδουπε, βαρύκτυπε, ἐννοσίγαιε,
5   κυμοθαλής, χαριδῶτα, τετράορον ἅρμα διώκων,
εἰναλίοις ῥοίζοισι τινάσσων ἁλμυρὸν ὕδωρ,
ὃς τριτάτης ἔλαχες μοίρης βαθὺ χεῦμα θαλάσσης,
κύμασι τερπόμενος θηρσίν θ᾽ ἅμα, πόντιε δαῖμον·

16. TO HERA,
incense - aromatic herbs

You are ensconced in darksome hollows, and airy is
    your form,
O Hera, queen of all and blessed consort of Zeus.
You send soft breezes to mortals, such as nourish
    the soul,
and, O mother of rains, you nurture the winds and
    give birth to all.
5   Without you there is neither life nor growth;
and, mixed as you are in the air we venerate, you
    partake of all,
and of all you are queen and mistress.
You toss and turn with the rushing wind.
May you, O blessed goddess and many-named queen of
    all,
10   come with kindness and joy on your lovely face.

17. TO POSEIDON,
incense - myrrh

Hearken, dark-maned Poseidon, holder of the earth,
equestrian; carved in bronze is the trident in your
    hand,
and you dwell in the foundations of the full-
    bosomed sea.
Deep-roaring ruler of the sea and shaker of the
    earth,
5   your blossoms are waves, O gracious one, as you
    urge horses and chariot on,
rushing on the sea and splashing through the
    rippling brine.
To your lot fell the third portion, the unfathomable
    sea,
and you delight in waves and in their wild dwellers,
    O spirit of the deep.

10   ἕδρανα γῆς σώζοις καὶ νηῶν εὔδρομον ὁρμήν,
     εἰρήνην, ὑγίειαν ἄγων ἠδ᾽ ὄλβον ἀμεμφῆ.

                18 Εἰς Πλούτωνα.

     Ὦ τὸν ὑποχθόνιον ναίων δόμον, ὀμβριμόθυμε,
     Ταρτάριον λειμῶνα βαθύσκιον ἠδὲ λιπαυγῆ,
     Ζεῦ χθόνιε, σκηπτοῦχε, τάδ᾽ ἱερὰ δέξο προθύμως,
     Πλούτων, ὃς κατέχεις γαίης κληῖδας ἁπάσης,
5   πλουτοδοτῶν γενεὴν βροτέην καρποῖς ἐνιαυτῶν·
     ὃς τριτάτης μοίρης ἔλαχες χθόνα παμβασίλειαν,
     ἕδρανον ἀθανάτων, θνητῶν στήριγμα κραταιόν·
     ὃς θρόνον ἐστήριξας ὑπὸ ζοφοειδέα χῶρον
     τηλέπορον τ᾽, ἀκάμαντα, λιπόπνοον, ἄκριτον Ἅιδην
10   κυάνεόν τ᾽ Ἀχέρονθ᾽, ὃς ἔχει ῥιζώματα γαίης·
     ὃς κρατέεις θνητῶν θανάτου χάριν, ὦ πολυδέγμων
     Εὔβουλ᾽, ἁγνοπόλου Δήμητερος ὅς ποτε παῖδα
     νυμφεύσας λειμῶνος ἀποσπαδίην διὰ πόντου
     τετρώροις ἵπποισιν ὑπ᾽ Ἀτθίδος ἤγαγες ἄντρον
15   δήμου Ἐλευσῖνος, τόθι περ πύλαι εἴσ᾽ Ἀίδαο.
     μοῦνος ἔφυς ἀφανῶν ἔργων φανερῶν τε βραβευτής,
     ἔνθεε, παντοκράτωρ, ἱερώτατε, ἀγλαότιμε,
     σεμνοῖς μυστιπόλοις χαίρων ὁσίοις τε σεβασμοῖς·
     ἵλαον ἀγκαλέω σε μολεῖν κεχαρηότα μύσταις.

Save the foundations of the earth and ships moving
    at full tilt,
10   and bring peace, health, and blameless prosperity.

18.   TO PLOUTON

Subterranean is your dwelling place, O strong-
    spirited one,
a meadow in Tartaros, thick-shaded and dark.
Chthonic Zeus, sceptered one, kindly accept this
    sacrifice,
Plouton, holder of the keys to the whole earth.
5   You give the wealth of the year's fruits to mankind,
and to your lot fell the third portion, earth,
    queen of all,
seat of the gods, mighty lap for mortals.
Your throne rests on a tenebrous realm,
the distant, untiring, windless and impassive Hades,
10   and on dark Acheron that encompasses the roots of
    the earth.
All-Receiver, with death at your command, you are
    master of mortals;
Euboulos, you once took pure Demeter's daughter as
    your bride
when you tore her away from the meadow and through
    the sea
upon your steeds you carried her to an Attic cave,
15   in the district of Eleusis, where the gates to
    Hades are.
You alone were born to judge deeds obscure and
    conspicuous;
holiest and illustrious ruler of all, frenzied god,
you delight in the worshiper's respect and
    reverence.
Come with favor and joy to the initiates.   I
    summon you.

19 Κεραυνοῦ Διός, θυμίαμα στύρακα.

Ζεῦ πάτερ, ὑψίδρομον πυραυγέα κόσμον ἐλαύνων,
στράπτων αἰθερίου στεροπῆς πανυπέρτατον αἴγλην,
παμμακάρων ἕδρανον θείαις βρονταῖσι τινάσσων,
νάμασι παννεφέλοις στεροπὴν φλεγέθουσαν ἀναίθων,
5 λαίλαπας, ὄμβρους, πρηστῆρας κρατερούς τε κεραυνούς,
βάλλων † ἐς ῥοθίους φλογερούς, βελέεσσι καλύπτων
παμφλέκτους, κρατερούς, φρικώδεας, ὀμβριμοθύμους,
πτηνὸν ὅπλον δεινόν, κλονοκάρδιον, ὀρθοέθειρον,
αἰφνίδιον, βρονταῖον, ἀνίκητον βέλος ἁγνὸν
10 ῥοίζου ἀπειρεσίου δινεύμασι, παμφάγον ὁρμῆι,
ἄρρηκτον, βαρύθυμον, ἀμαιμάκετον πρηστῆρος
οὐράνιον βέλος ὀξὺ καταιβάτου αἰθαλόεντος,
ὃν καὶ γαῖα πέφρικε θάλασσά τε παμφανόωντα,
καὶ θῆρες πτήσσουσιν, ὅταν κτύπος οὖας ἐσέλθηι·
15 μαρμαίρει δὲ πρόσωπ' αὐγαῖς, σμαραγεῖ δὲ κεραυνὸς
αἰθέρος ἐν γυάλοισι· διαρρήξας δὲ χιτῶνα
οὐράνιον προκάλυμμα † βάλλεις ἀργῆτα κεραυνόν.
ἀλλά, μάκαρ, θυμὸν [⏝⏝ 4 ⏝⏝] κύμασι πόντου
ἠδ' ὀρέων κορυφαῖσι· τὸ σὸν κράτος ἴσμεν ἅπαντες.
20 ἀλλὰ χαρεὶς λοιβαῖσι δίδου φρεσὶν αἴσιμα πάντα
ζωήν τ' ὀλβιόθυμον, ὁμοῦ θ' ὑγίειαν ἄνασσαν
εἰρήνην τε θεόν, κουροτρόφον, ἀγλαότιμον,
καὶ βίον εὐθύμοισιν ἀεὶ θάλλοντα λογισμοῖς.

19. TO ZEUS THE THUNDERBOLT

incense - storax

Father Zeus, sublime is the course of the blazing
    cosmos you drive on,
and ethereal and lofty the flash of your lightning,
as you shake the seat of the immortals with divine
    thunderbolts.
With the fire of your lightning you emblazon the
    rain clouds;
5   storms you bring and hurricanes, and mighty
    thunder,
blazing and roaring thunder - like a shower of
    arrows -
which with horrific might and strength sets all
    aflame,
this dreadful missile that makes hearts pound and
    hair bristle.
Holy and invincible, it comes with a sudden crash,
10   an endless spiral of noise, omnivorous in its
    drive,
unbreakable, threatening, and ineluctable; the
    gale's
sharp and smoke-filled shaft swoops down
with a flash, dreaded by land and sea.
Wild beasts cringe when they hear the noise,
15   faces reflect the brilliance of thunder roaring
in the celestial hollows. You tear the robe
that cloaks heaven and hurl the fiery thunderbolt.
But, O blessed one, (calm down?) the anger of sea
    waves
and mountain peaks. We all know your power.
20   Enjoy this libation and give all things that
    please the heart,
a life of prosperity, queenly health,
divine peace that nurtures youths and is with
    honors crowned,
and an existence ever blooming with cheerful
    thoughts.

20 Διὸς Ἀστραπαίου, θυμίαμα λιβανομάνναν.

Κικλήσκω μέγαν, ἁγνόν, ἐρισμάραγον, περίφαντον,
ἀέριον, φλογόεντα, πυρίδρομον, ἀεροφεγγῆ,
ἀστράπτοντα σέλας νεφέων παταγοδρόμωι αὐδῆι,
φρικώδη, βαρύμηνιν, ἀνίκητον θεὸν ἁγνόν,
5   ἀστραπαῖον Δία, παγγενέτην, βασιλῆα μέγιστον,
εὐμενέοντα φέρειν γλυκερὴν βιότοιο τελευτήν.

21 Νεφῶν, θυμίαμα σμύρναν.

Ἀέριοι νεφέλαι, καρποτρόφοι, οὐρανόπλαγκτοι,
ὀμβροτόκοι, πνοιαῖσιν ἐλαυνόμεναι κατὰ κόσμον,
βρονταῖαι, πυρόεσσαι, ἐρίβρομοι, ὑγροκέλευθοι,
ἀέρος ἐν κόλπωι πάταγον φρικώδη ἔχουσαι,
5   πνεύμασιν ἀντίσπαστοι ἐπιδρομάδην παταγεῦσαι,
ὑμᾶς νῦν λίτομαι, δροσοείμονες, εὔπνοοι αὔραις,
πέμπειν καρποτρόφους ὄμβρους ἐπὶ μητέρα γαῖαν.

22 Θαλάσσης, θυμίαμα λιβανομάνναν.

Ὠκεανοῦ καλέω νύμφην, γλαυκώπιδα Τηθύν,
κυανόπεπλον ἄνασσαν, εὔτροχα κυμαίνουσαν,
αὔραις ἡδυπνόοισι πατασσομένην περὶ γαῖαν.
θραύουσ᾽ αἰγιαλοῖσι πέτρηισί τε κύματα μακρά,
5   εὐδίνοις ἀπαλοῖσι γαληνιόωσα δρόμοισι,

20. TO ASTRAPAIOS ZEUS,
incense - powdered frankincense

I call upon great, pure, resounding, illustrious,
ethereal and blazing Zeus, whose racing fire
    shines through the air.
With an ear-splitting clap your light flashes
    through the clouds,
O horrid, wrathful, pure, and invincible god.
5 Upon you I call, lord of lightning, begetter of
    all and great king,
to be kind and bring a sweet end to my life.

21. TO THE CLOUDS,
incense - myrrh

Airy clouds that nourish fruits and rove the sky,
you give rain as you are driven everywhere by the
    wind.
Filled with blazing thunder and water, you resound
with awesome crashes in the air-filled vault of
    heaven
5 when you are repelled by the onrush of raging
    winds.
To you I pray, you whose dewy cloaks are blown by
    fair breezes,
to send fruit-nourishing rains to mother earth.

22. TO THE SEA,
incense - pounded frankincense

I call upon gray-eyed Tethys, bride of Okeanos,
dark-veiled queen, whose waves dance
as they are blown onto the land by the sweet
    breezes.
You break your tall waves upon rocky beaches,
5 and you are calmed by races that are gentle and
    smooth.

ναυσὶν ἀγαλλομένη, θηροτρόφε, ὑγροκέλευθε,
μήτηρ μὲν Κύπριδος, μήτηρ νεφέων ἐρεβεννῶν
καὶ πάσης πηγῆς νυμφῶν νασμοῖσι βρυούσης·
κλῦθί μου, ὦ πολύσεμνε, καὶ εὐμενέουσ᾽ ἐπαρήγοις,
εὐθυδρόμοις οὖρον ναυσὶν πέμπουσα, μάκαιρα.

23 Νηρέως, θυμίαμα σμύρναν.

Ὦ κατέχων πόντου ῥίζας, κυαναυγέτιν ἕδρην,
πεντήκοντα κόραισιν ἀγαλλόμενος κατὰ κῦμα
καλλιτέκνοισι χοροῖς, Νηρεῦ, μεγαλώνυμε δαῖμον,
πυθμὴν μὲν πόντου, γαίης πέρας, ἀρχὴ ἁπάντων,
5 ὃς κλονέεις Δηοῦς ἱερὸν βάθρον, ἡνίκα πνοιὰς
ἐννυχίοις κευθμῶσιν ἐλαυνομένας ἀποκλείηις·
ἀλλά, μάκαρ, σεισμοὺς μὲν ἀπότρεπε, πέμπε δὲ μύσταις
ὄλβον τ᾽ εἰρήνην τε καὶ ἠπιόχειρον ὑγείην.

24 Νηρηίδων, θυμίαμα ἀρώματα.

Νηρέος εἰναλίου νύμφαι καλυκώπιδες, ἁγναί,
† σφράγιαι βύθιαι, χοροπαίγμονες, ὑγροκέλευθοι,
πεντήκοντα κόραι περὶ κύμασι βακχεύουσαι,
Τριτώνων ἐπ᾽ ὄχοισιν ἀγαλλόμεναι περὶ νῶτα
5 θηροτύποις μορφαῖς, ὧν βόσκει σώματα πόντος,
ἄλλοις θ᾽ οἳ ναίουσι βυθόν, Τριτώνιον οἶδμα,

You delight in ships and your waters feed wild
    beasts,
mother of Kypris, mother of dark clouds
and of every spring round which nymphs swarm.
Hear me, O holy one, kindly help,
10   and, blessed one, send a fair tail wind to ships.

23. TO NEREUS,
incense - myrrh

The sea's foundations are your realm, an abode of
    glossy blackness,
and you exult in the beauty of your fifty
    daughters
as they dance amid the waves. O Nereus, god of
    great renown,
foundation of the sea, end of the earth, beginning
    of all,
5   you make Demeter's sacred throne tremble when you
    imprison
the gusty winds driven to your gloomy depths.
But, O blessed one, ward off earthquakes, and send
to the initiates peace, prosperity and gentle-
    handed health.

24. TO THE NEREIDS,
incense - aromatic herbs

O lovely-faced and pure nymphs, daughters of Nereus
    who lives in the deep,
at the bottom of the sea you gambol and dance in
    the water.
Fifty maidens revel in the waves,
maidens riding on the backs of Tritons and
    delighting
5   in animal shapes and bodies nurtured by the sea
and in the other dwellers of the Tritons' billowy
    kingdom.

ὑδρόδομοι, σκιρτηταί, ἑλισσόμενοι περὶ κῦμα,
ποντοπλάνοι δελφῖνες, ἁλιρρόθιοι, κυαναυγεῖς.
ὑμᾶς κικλήσκω πέμπειν μύσταις πολὺν ὄλβον·
10   ὑμεῖς γὰρ πρῶται τελετὴν ἀνεδείξατε σεμνὴν
εὐιέρου Βάκχοιο καὶ ἁγνῆς Φερσεφονείης,
Καλλιόπηι σὺν μητρὶ καὶ Ἀπόλλωνι ἄνακτι.

25 Πρωτέως, θυμίαμα στύρακα.

Πρωτέα κικλήσκω, πόντου κληῖδας ἔχοντα,
πρωτογενῆ, πάσης φύσεως ἀρχὰς ὃς ἔφηνεν
ὕλην ἀλλάσσων ἱερὴν ἰδέαις πολυμόρφοις,
πάντιμος, πολύβουλος, ἐπιστάμενος τά τ᾽ ἐόντα
5   ὅσσα τε πρόσθεν ἔην ὅσα τ᾽ ἔσσεται ὕστερον αὖτις·
πάντα γὰρ αὐτὸς ἔχων μεταβάλλεται οὐδέ τις ἄλλος
ἀθανάτων, οἳ ἔχουσιν ἕδος νιφόεντος Ὀλύμπου
καὶ πόντον καὶ γαῖαν ἐνηέριοί τε ποτῶνται·
† πάντα γὰρ † Πρωτεῖ πρώτη φύσις ἐγκατέθηκε.
10   ἀλλά, πάτερ, μόλε μυστιπόλοις ὁσίαισι προνοίαις
πέμπων εὐόλβου βιότου τέλος ἐσθλὸν ἐπ᾽ ἔργοις.

26 Γῆς, θυμίαμα πᾶν σπέρμα πλὴν κυάμων καὶ ἀρωμάτων.

Γαῖα θεά, μῆτερ μακάρων θνητῶν τ᾽ ἀνθρώπων,
παντρόφε, πανδώτειρα, τελεσφόρε, παντολέτειρα,
αὐξιθαλής, φερέκαρπε, καλαῖς ὥραισι βρύουσα,

Your home is the water, and you leap and whirl
   round the waves,
like glistening dolphins roving the roaring seas.
I call upon you to bring much prosperity to the
   initiates,
10   for you were first to show the holy rite
of sacred Bacchos and of pure Persephone,
you and mother Kalliope, and Apollon the lord.

25. TO PROTEUS,
incense - storax

I call upon Proteus, key-holding master of the sea,
first-born, who showed the beginnings of all
   nature,
changing matter into a great variety of forms.
Honored by all, he is wise and knows what is now,
5   what was before, and what will be in the future.
He has all at his disposal and he is transformed
   far beyond
the other immortals who dwell on snowy Olympos
and fly through the air and over land and sea,
for nature was the first to place everything in
   Proteus.
10   But, father, attended by holy providence visit the
   mystic initiates
and bring a good end to a life of industry and
   prosperity.

26. TO EARTH,
incense and any grain save
beans and aromatic herbs

Divine Earth, mother of men and of the blessed
   gods,
you nourish all, you give all, you bring all to
   fruition, and you destroy all.
When the season is fair you are heavy with fruit
   and growing blossoms;

38

ἕδρανον ἀθανάτου κόσμου, πολυποίκιλε κούρη,
ἢ λοχίαις ὠδῖσι κύεις καρπὸν πολυειδῆ,
ἀιδία, πολύσεπτε, βαθύστερν᾽, ὀλβιόμοιρε,
ἡδυπνόοις χαίρουσα χλόαις πολυανθέσι δαῖμον,
ὀμβροχαρής, περὶ ἣν κόσμος πολυδαίδαλος ἄστρων
εἰλεῖται φύσει ἀενάωι καὶ ῥεύμασι δεινοῖς.
ἀλλά, μάκαιρα θεά, καρποὺς αὔξοις πολυγηθεῖς
εὐμενὲς ἦτορ ἔχουσα, † σὺν ὀλβίοισιν † ἐν ὥραις.

27 Μητρὸς θεῶν, θυμίαμα ποικίλα.

Ἀθανάτων θεότιμε θεῶν μῆτερ, τροφὲ πάντων,
τῆιδε μόλοις, κράντειρα θεά, σέο, πότνι᾽, ἐπ᾽ εὐχαῖς,
ταυροφόνων ζεύξασα ταχυδρόμον ἅρμα λεόντων,
σκηπτοῦχε κλεινοῖο πόλου, πολυώνυμε, σεμνή,
ἢ κατέχεις κόσμοιο μέσον θρόνον, οὕνεκεν αὐτὴ
γαῖαν ἔχεις θνητοῖσι τροφὰς παρέχουσα προσηνεῖς.
ἐκ σέο δ᾽ ἀθανάτων τε γένος θνητῶν τ᾽ ἐλοχεύθη,
σοὶ ποταμοὶ κρατέονται ἀεὶ καὶ πᾶσα θάλασσα,
Ἑστία αὐδαχθεῖσα· σὲ δ᾽ ὀλβοδότιν καλέουσι,
παντοίων ἀγαθῶν θνητοῖς ὅτι δῶρα χαρίζηι,
ἔρχεο πρὸς τελετήν, ὦ πότνια, τυμπανοτερπή⟨ς⟩,
πανδαμάτωρ, Φρυγίη⟨ς⟩, σώτειρα, Κρόνου συνόμευνε,
Οὐρανόπαι, πρέσβειρα, βιοθρέπτειρα, φίλοιστρε·
ἔρχεο γηθόσυνος, κεχαρισμένη εὐσεβίηισιν.

and, O multiform maiden, you are the seat of the
      immortal cosmos,
5   and in the pains of labor you bring forth fruit of
      all kinds.
Eternal, reverend, deep-bosomed, and blessed,
you delight in the sweet breath of grass, O goddess
      bedecked with flowers.
Yours is the joy of the rain, and round you the
      intricate realm of the stars
revolves in endless and awesome flow.
10   But, O blessed goddess, may you multiply the glad-
      some fruits
and, together with the beautiful seasons, grant me
      favor.

27. TO THE MOTHER OF THE GODS,
                           incense - et varia

Divine are your honors, O mother of the gods and
      nurturer of all.
Yoke your swift chariot drawn by bull-slaying lions
and, O mighty goddess who brings things to pass,
      join our prayers.
Many-named and reverend, you are queen of the sky,
5   for in the cosmos yours is the throne in the middle
      because
the earth is yours and you give gentle nourishment
      to mortals.
Gods and men were born of you,
and you hold sway over the rivers and all the sea.
Hestia is one of your names, and they call you
      giver of prosperity
10   because you bestow on men all manner of gifts.
Come to this rite, queen whom the drum delights,
all-taming, savior of Phrygia, consort of Kronos,
child of Ouranos, honored and frenzy-loving
      nurturer of life.
Joyously and graciously visit our deeds of piety.

28 Ἑρμοῦ, θυμίαμα λίβανον.

Κλῦθί μου, Ἑρμεία, Διὸς ἄγγελε, Μαιάδος υἱέ,
παγκρατὲς ἦτορ ἔχων, ἐναγώνιε, κοίρανε θνητῶν,
εὔφρων, ποικιλόβουλε, διάκτορε ἀργειφόντα,
πτηνοπέδιλε, φίλανδρε, λόγου θνητοῖσι προφῆτα,
5   γυμνάσιν ὃς χαίρεις δολίαις τ' ἀπάταις, † τροφιοῦχε,
ἑρμηνεῦ πάντων, κερδέμπορε, λυσιμέριμνε,
ὃς χείρεσσιν ἔχεις εἰρήνης ὅπλον ἀμεμφές,
Κωρυκιῶτα, μάκαρ, ἐριούνιε, ποικιλόμυθε,
ἐργασίαις ἐπαρωγέ, φίλε θνητοῖς ἐν ἀνάγκαις,
10   γλώσσης δεινὸν ὅπλον τὸ σεβάσμιον ἀνθρώποισι·
κλῦθί μου εὐχομένου, βιότου τέλος ἐσθλὸν ὀπάζων
ἐργασίαισι, λόγου χάρισιν καὶ μνημοσύνῃσιν.

29 Ὕμνος Περσεφόνης.

Φερσεφόνη, θύγατερ μεγάλου Διός, ἐλθέ, μάκαιρα,
μουνογένεια θεά, κεχαρισμένα δ' ἱερὰ δέξαι,
Πλούτωνος πολύτιμε δάμαρ, κεδνή, βιοδῶτι,
ἣ κατέχεις Ἀίδαο πύλας ὑπὸ κεύθεα γαίης,
5   Πραξιδίκη, ἐρατοπλόκαμε, Δηοῦς θάλος ἁγνόν,
Εὐμενίδων γενέτειρα, ὑποχθονίων βασίλεια,
ἣν Ζεὺς ἀρρήτοισι γοναῖς τεκνώσατο κούρην,

28. TO HERMES,
incense - frankincense

Hear me, Hermes, messenger of Zeus, son of Maia;
almighty is your heart, O lord of the deceased and
    judge of contests;
gentle and clever, O Argeiphontes, you are a guide
whose sandals fly, and a man-loving prophet to
    mortals.
5   You are vigorous and you delight in exercise and
    in deceit;
interpreter of all, you are a profiteer who frees
    us of cares
and who holds in his hands the blameless tool of
    peace.
Lord of Korykos, blessed, helpful and skilled in
    words,
you assist in work, you are a friend of mortals in
    need,
10   and you wield the dreaded and respected weapon of
    speech.
Hear my prayer and grant a good end to a life
of industry, gracious talk, and mindfulness.

29. HYMN TO PERSEPHONE

Persephone, blessed daughter of great Zeus, sole
    offspring
of Demeter, come and accept this gracious
    sacrifice.
Much honored spouse of Plouton, discreet and life-
    giving,
you command the gates of Hades in the bowels of
    the earth,
5   lovely-tressed Praxidike, pure bloom of Deo,
mother of the Furies, queen of the nether world,
whom Zeus sired in clandestine union.

10

μῆτερ ἐριβρεμέτου πολυμόρφου Εὐβουλῆος,
Ὡρῶν συμπαίκτειρα, φαεσφόρε, ἀγλαόμορφε,
σεμνή, παντοκράτειρα, κόρη καρποῖσι βρύουσα,
εὐφεγγής, κερόεσσα, μόνη θνητοῖσι ποθεινή,
εἰαρινή, λειμωνιάσιν χαίρουσα πνοῆισιν,
ἱερὸν ἐκφαίνουσα δέμας βλαστοῖς χλοοκάρποις,
ἁρπαγιμαῖα λέχη μετοπωρινὰ νυμφευθεῖσα,

15

ζωὴ καὶ θάνατος μούνη θνητοῖς πολυμόχθοις,
Φερσεφόνη· φέρβεις γὰρ ἀεὶ καὶ πάντα φονεύεις.
κλῦθι, μάκαιρα θεά, καρποὺς δ᾽ ἀνάπεμπ᾽ ἀπὸ γαίης
εἰρήνηι θάλλουσα καὶ ἠπιοχείρωι ὑγείαι
καὶ βίωι εὐόλβωι λιπαρὸν γῆρας κατάγοντι

20

πρὸς σὸν χῶρον, ἄνασσα, καὶ εὐδύνατον Πλούτωνα.

30 Διονύσου, θυμίαμα στύρακα.

Κικλήσκω Διόνυσον ἐρίβρομον, εὐαστῆρα,
πρωτόγονον, διφυῆ, τρίγονον, Βακχεῖον ἄνακτα,
ἄγριον, ἄρρητον, κρύφιον, δικέρωτα, δίμορφον,
κισσόβρυον, ταυρωπόν, Ἀρήιον, εὔιον, ἁγνόν,

5

ὠμάδιον, τριετῆ, βοτρυηφόρον, ἐρνεσίπεπλον.
Εὐβουλεῦ, πολύβουλε, Διὸς καὶ Περσεφονείης
ἀρρήτοις λέκτροισι τεκνωθείς, ἄμβροτε δαῖμον·
κλῦθι, μάκαρ, φωνῆς, ἡδὺς δ᾽ ἐπίπνευσον ἀμεμ[φ]ής
εὐμενὲς ἦτορ ἔχων, σὺν ἐυζώνοισι τιθήναις.

Mother of loud-roaring and many-shaped Eubouleus,
radiant and luminous playmate of the Seasons,
10   august, almighty, maiden rich in fruits,
brilliant and horned, you alone are beloved of
        mortals.
In spring you rejoice in the meadow breezes
and you show your holy figure in shoots and green
        fruits.
You were made a kidnapper's bride in the fall,
15   and you alone are life and death to toiling
        mortals,
O Persephone, for you always nourish all and kill
        them, too.
Hearken, O blessed goddess, and send forth the
        earth's fruits.
You who blossom in peace, in soft-handed health,
and in a life of plenty that ferries old age in
        comfort
20   to your realm, O queen, and to that of mighty
        Plouton.

30.   TO DIONYSOS,
                        incense - storax

I call upon loud-roaring and reveling Dionysos,
primeval, two-natured, thrice-born, Bacchic lord,
savage, ineffable, secretive, two-horned and two-
        shaped.
Ivy-covered, bull-faced, warlike, howling, pure,
5   you take raw flesh, you have triennial feasts,
        wrapt in foliage, decked with grape clusters.
Resourceful Eubouleus, immortal god sired by Zeus
when he mated with Persephone in unspeakable union.
Hearken to my voice, O blessed one, and with your
        fair-girdled nurses
breathe on me in a spirit of perfect kindness.

44

31 Ὕμνος Κουρήτων.

Σκιρτηταὶ Κουρῆτες, ἐνόπλια βήματα θέντες,
ποσσίκροτοι, ῥομβηταί, ὀρέστεροι, εὐαστῆρες,
κρουσιλύραι, παράρυθμοι, ἐπεμβάται, ἴχνεσι κοῦφοι,
ὁπλοφόροι, φύλακες, κοσμήτορες, ἀγλαόφημοι,
5 μητρὸς ὀρειομανοῦς συνοπάονες, ὀργιοφάνται·
ἔλθοιτ᾽ εὐμενέοντες ἐπ᾽ εὐφήμοισι λόγοισι,
βουκόλωι εὐάντητοι ἀεὶ κεχαρηότι θυμῶι.

32 Ἀθηνᾶς, θυμίαμα ἀρώματα.

Παλλὰς μουνογενή⟨ς⟩, μεγάλου Διὸς ἔκγονε σεμνή,
δῖα, μάκαιρα θεά, πολεμόκλονε, ὀμβριμόθυμε,
ἄρρητε, ῥητή, μεγαλώνυμε, ἀντροδίαιτε,
ἣ διέπεις ὄχθους ὑψαύχενας ἀκρωρείους
5 ἠδ᾽ ὄρεα σκιόεντα, νάπαισί τε σὴν φρένα τέρπεις,
ὁπλοχαρής, οἰστροῦσα βροτῶν ψυχὰς μανίαισι,
γυμνάζουσα κόρη, φρικώδη θυμὸν ἔχουσα,
Γοργοφόνη, φυγόλεκτρε, τεχνῶν μῆτερ πολύολβε,
ὁρμάστειρα, φίλοιστρε κακοῖς, ἀγαθοῖς δὲ φρόνησις·
10 ἄρσην μὲν καὶ θῆλυς ἔφυς, πολεματόκε, μῆτι,
αἰολόμορφε, δράκαινα, φιλένθεε, ἀγλαότιμε,
Φλεγραίων ὀλέτειρα Γιγάντων, ἱππελάτειρα,
Τριτογένεια, λύτειρα κακῶν, νικηφόρε δαῖμον,
ἤματα καὶ νύκτας αἰεὶ νεάταισιν ἐν ὥραις,

31. HYMN TO THE KOURETES

Leaping Kouretes, stepping to the sound of arms,
howling mountaineers, whose feet pound the ground,
discordant is the lyre you strike as you pace,
    light of foot,
O renowned marshals and arm-carrying guards,

5   priests in the train of a mother struck with
    mountain frenzy.
Kindly visit those whose words praise you
and, with joyous heart, be gracious to the oxherd.

32. TO ATHENA,
incense - aromatic herbs

Revered Pallas, you alone great Zeus bore by him-
    self,
noble and blessed goddess, brave in the din of war.
Renowned and cave-haunting, you may and may not be
    spoken of.
Your domain is on wind-swept hilltops

5   and shaded mountains, and dells charm your heart.
Arms please you, and you strike men's souls with
    frenzy,
O maiden vigorous and horrid-tempered.
Slayer of Gorgo, blessed mother of the arts, you
    shun the bed of love
and, O impetuous one, you bring madness to the
    wicked and prudence to the virtuous.

10   Male and female, begetter of war, counselor,
she-dragon of many shapes, frenzy-loving,
    illustrious,
destroyer of the Phlegraian Giants, driver of
    horses,
Tritogeneia, you free us of suffering, O victorious
    goddess.
Day and night - ever into the small hours -

¹⁵ κλῦθί μου εὐχομένου, δὸς δ' εἰρήνην πολύολβον
καὶ κόρον ἠδ' ὑγίειαν † ἐπ' εὐόλβοισιν † ἐν ὥραις,
γλαυκῶφ', εὑρεσίτεχνε, πολυλλίστη βασίλεια.

33 Νίκης, θυμίαμα μάνναν.

Εὐδύνατον καλέω Νίκην, θνητοῖσι ποθεινήν,
ἢ μούνη λύει θνητῶν ἐναγώνιον ὁρμὴν
καὶ στάσιν ἀλγινόεσσαν ἐπ' ἀντιπάλοισι μάχαισιν,
ἐν πολέμοις κρίνουσα τροπαιούχοισιν ἐπ' ἔργοις,
⁵ οἷς ἂν ἐφορμαίνουσα φέροις γλυκερώτατον εὖχος·
πάντων γὰρ κρατέεις, πάσης δ' ἔριδος κλέος ἐσθλὸν
Νίκηι ἐπ' εὐδόξωι κεῖται θαλίαισι βρυάζον.
ἀλλά, μάκαιρ', ἔλθοις πεποθημένη ὄμματι φαιδρῶι
αἰεὶ ἐπ' εὐδόξοις ἔργοις τέλος ἐσθλὸν ἄγουσα.

34 Ἀπόλλωνος, θυμίαμα μάνναν.

Ἐλθέ, μάκαρ, Παιάν, Τιτυοκτόνε, Φοῖβε, Λυκωρεῦ,
Μεμφῖτ', ἀγλαότιμε, ἰήιε, ὀλβιοδῶτα,
χρυσολύρη, σπερμεῖε, ἀρότριε, Πύθιε, Τιτάν,
Γρύνειε, Σμινθεῦ, Πυθοκτόνε, Δελφικέ, μάντι,
⁵ ἄγριε, φωσφόρε δαῖμον, ἐράσμιε, κύδιμε κοῦρε,

15   hear my prayer and give me a full measure of peace,
of riches, and of health accompanied by happy
   seasons,
O gray-eyed and inventive queen to whom many pray.

33. TO NIKE,
incense - powdered frank-
incense

I call upon mighty Nike, beloved of mortals,
for she alone frees man from the eagerness for
   contest
and from dissent when men face each other in
   battle.
In war you are the judge of deeds deserving prizes,
5   and sweet is the boast you grant after the
   onslaught.
Nike, mistress of all, on you and your good name
   depends noble glory,
glory that comes from strife and teems with
   festivities.
But, O blessed and beloved one, come with joy in
   your eyes,
come for works of renown, and bring me a noble end.

34. TO APOLLON,
incense - powdered frankincense

Come, O blessed Paian, O slayer of Tityos, O
   Phoibos, O Lykoreus;
A giver of riches are you and an illustrious
   dweller of Memphis, O god to whom one cries ie.
To you, O Titan and Pythian god, belong the lyre,
   and seeds and plows.
Grynean, Sminthian, slayer of Pytho, Delphic
   diviner,
5   you are a wild, light-bringing and lovable god,
   O glorious youth.

† μουσαγέτα, χοροποιέ, ἐκηβόλε, τοξοβέλεμνε,
Βάκχιε καὶ Διδυμεῦ, † ἑκάεργε, Λοξία, ἁγνέ,
Δήλι᾽ ἄναξ, πανδερκὲς ἔχων φαεσίμβροτον ὄμμα,
χρυσοκόμα, καθαρὰς φήμας χρησμούς τ᾽ ἀναφαίνων·
10 κλῦθί μου εὐχομένου λαῶν ὕπερ εὔφρονι θυμῶι·
τόνδε σὺ γὰρ λεύσσεις τὸν ἀπείριτον αἰθέρα πάντα
γαῖάν τ᾽ ὀλβιόμοιρον †ὕπερθέ τε† καὶ δι᾽ ἀμολγοῦ,
νυκτὸς ἐν ἡσυχίαισιν ὑπ᾽ ἀστεροόμματον ὄρφνην
ῥίζας νέρθε δέδορκας, ἔχεις δέ τε πείρατα κόσμου
15 παντός· σοὶ δ᾽ ἀρχή τε τελευτή τ᾽ ἐστὶ μέλουσα,
παντοθαλής, σὺ δὲ πάντα πόλον κιθάρηι πολυκρέκτωι
ἁρμόζεις, ὁτὲ μὲν νεάτης ἐπὶ τέρματα βαίνων,
ἄλλοτε δ᾽ αὖθ᾽ ὑπάτην, ποτὲ Δώριον εἰς διάκοσμον
πάντα πόλον κιρνὰς κρίνεις βιοθρέμμονα φῦλα,
20 ἁρμονίηι κεράσας {τὴν} παγκόσμιον ἀνδράσι μοῖραν,
μίξας χειμῶνος θέρεός τ᾽ ἴσον ἀμφοτέροισιν,
εἰς ὑπάτας χειμῶνα, θέρος νεάταις διακρίνας,
Δώριον εἰς ἔαρος πολυηράτου ὥριον ἄνθος.

ἔνθεν ἐπωνυμίην σε βροτοὶ κλήιζουσιν ἄνακτα,
25 Πᾶνα, θεὸν δικέρωτ᾽, ἀνέμων συρίγμαθ᾽ ἱέντα·
οὕνεκα παντὸς ἔχεις κόσμου σφραγῖδα τυπῶτιν.
κλῦθι, μάκαρ, σώζων μύστας ἱκετηρίδι φωνῆι.

You shoot your arrows from afar, you lead the
   Muses into dance,
and, O holy one, you are Bacchos, Didymeus, and
   Loxias, too.
Lord of Delos, eye that sees all and brings light
   to mortals,
golden is your hair, and clear your oracular
   utterance.
10   Hear me with kindly heart as I pray for people.
You gaze upon all the ethereal vastness,
and upon the rich earth you look through the
   twilight.
In the quiet darkness of a night lit with stars
you see earth's roots below, and you hold the
   bounds
15   of the whole world. Yours, too, are the beginning
   and the end to come.
You make everything bloom, and with your versatile
   lyre
you harmonize the poles, now reaching the highest
   pitch,
now the lowest, and now again with the Doric mode
balancing the poles harmoniously, as you keep the
   living races distinct.
20   You have infused harmony into all men's lot,
giving them an equal measure of summer and winter.
The lowest notes you strike in the winter, the
   highest in the summer,
and your mode is Doric for spring's lovely and
   blooming season.
Wherefore mortals call you lord, and Pan,
25   the two-horned god who sends the whistling winds.
For this, too, you have the master seal of the
   entire cosmos.
O blessed one, hear the suppliant voice of the
   initiates and save them.

35 Λητοῦς, θυμίαμα σμύρναν.

Λητὼ κυανόπεπλε, θεὰ διδυματόκε, σεμνή,
Κοιαντίς, μεγάθυμε, πολυλλίστη βασίλεια,
εὔτεκνον Ζηνὸς γονίμην ὠδῖνα λαχοῦσα,
γειναμένη Φοῖβόν τε καὶ Ἄρτεμιν ἰοχέαιραν,
5 τὴν μὲν ἐν Ὀρτυγίηι, τὸν δὲ κραναῆι ἐνὶ Δήλωι,
κλῦθι, θεὰ δέσποινα, καὶ ἵλαον ἦτορ ἔχουσα
βαῖν' ἐπὶ πάνθειον τελετὴν τέλος ἡδὺ φέρουσα.

36 Ἀρτέμιδος, θυμίαμα μάνναν.

Κλῦθί μου, ὦ βασίλεια, Διὸς πολυώνυμε κούρη,
Τιτανίς, βρομία, μεγαλώνυμε, τοξότι, σεμνή,
πασιφαής, δαιδοῦχε θεά, Δίκτυννα, λοχεία,
ὠδίνων ἐπαρωγὲ καὶ ὠδίνων ἀμύητε,
5 λυσίζωνε, φίλοιστρε, κυνηγέτι, λυσιμέριμνε,
εὔδρομε, ἰοχέαιρα, φιλαγρότι, νυκτερόφοιτε,
κληισία, εὐάντητε, λυτηρία, ἀρσενόμορφε,
Ὀρθία, ὠκυλόχεια, βροτῶν κουροτρόφε δαῖμον,
ἀμβροτέρα, χθονία, θηροκτόνε, ὀλβιόμοιρε,
10 ἣ κατέχεις ὀρέων δρυμούς, ἐλαφηβόλε, σεμνή,
πότνια, παμβασίλεια, καλὸν θάλος, αἰὲν ἐοῦσα,
δρυμονία, σκυλακῖτι, Κυδωνιάς, αἰολόμορφε·

35. TO LETO,
incense - myrrh

Dark-veiled Leto, revered goddess and mother
  of twins,
great-souled daughter of Koios, queen to whom
  many pray,
to your lot fell the birth pains for Zeus' fair
  child.
You bore Phoibos and arrow-pouring Artemis,
5   her on Ortygia and him on rocky Delos.
Hear, lady goddess, and with favor in your heart
come to this all-holy rite and bring sweet end.

36. TO ARTEMIS,
incense - powdered frankincense

Hear me, O queen, Zeus' daughter of many names,
Titanic and Bacchic, reverend, renowned archer,
torch-bearing goddess bringing light to all,
  Diktynna, helper at childbirth.
You aid women in labor, though you know not what
  labor is.
5   O frenzy-loving huntress, you loosen girdles and
  drive cares away;
swift, arrow-pouring, you love the outdoors and
  you roam in the night.
Fame-bringing, affable, redeeming, mannish,
Orthia, goddess of swift birth, nurturer of
  mortal youths.
Immortal and yet of this earth, you slay wild
  beasts, O blessed one,
10   and your realm is in the mountain forests. You
  hunt deer,
O august and mighty queen of all, fair blossom,
  eternal,
sylvan, dog-loving, many-shaped lady of Kydonia.

ἐλθέ, θεὰ σώτειρα, φίλη, μύστησιν ἅπασιν
εὐάντητος, ἄγουσα καλοὺς καρποὺς ἀπὸ γαίης
εἰρήνην τ’ ἐρατὴν καλλιπλόκαμόν θ’ ὑγίειαν·
πέμποις δ’ εἰς ὀρέων κεφαλὰς νούσους τέ καὶ ἄλγη.

37 Τιτάνων, θυμίαμα λίβανον.

Τιτῆνες, Γαίης τε καὶ Οὐρανοῦ ἀγλαὰ τέκνα,
ἡμετέρων πρόγονοι πατέρων, γαίης ὑπένερθεν
οἴκοις Ταρταρίοισι μυχῶι χθονὸς ἐνναίοντες,
ἀρχαὶ καὶ πηγαὶ πάντων θνητῶν πολυμόχθων,
εἰναλίων πτηνῶν τε καὶ οἳ χθόνα ναιετάουσιν·
ἐξ ὑμέων γὰρ πᾶσα πέλει γενεὰ κατὰ κόσμον.
ὑμᾶς κικλήσκω μῆνιν χαλεπὴν ἀποπέμπειν,
εἴ τις ἀπὸ χθονίων προγόνων οἴκοις ἐπελάσθη.

38 Κουρήτων, θυμίαμα λίβανον.

Χαλκόκροτοι Κουρῆτες, Ἀρήια τεύχε’ ἔχοντες,
οὐράνιοι χθόνιοί τε καὶ εἰνάλιοι, πολύολβοι,
Ζωιογόνοι πνοιαί, κόσμου σωτῆρες ἀγαυοί,
οἵτε Σαμοθράικην, ἱερὴν χθόνα, ναιετάοντες
κινδύνους θνητῶν ἀπερύκετε ποντοπλανήτων·
ὑμεῖς καὶ τελετὴν πρῶτοι μερόπεσσιν ἔθεσθε,
ἀθάνατοι Κουρῆτες, Ἀρήια τεύχε’ ἔχοντες·
νωμᾶτ’ Ὠκεανόν, νωμᾶθ’ ἅλα δένδρεά θ’ αὔτως·
ἐρχόμενοι γαῖαν κοναβίζετε ποσσὶν ἐλαφροῖς,
μαρμαίροντες ὅπλοις· πτήσσουσι δὲ θῆρες ἅπαντες
ὁρμώντων, θόρυβος δὲ βοή τ’ εἰς οὐρανὸν ἵκει
εἰλιγμοῖς τε ποδῶν κονίη νεφέλας ἀφικάνει
ἐρχομένων· τότε δή ῥα καὶ ἄνθεα πάντα τέθηλε.

Come, dear goddess, as savior, accessible to all
the initiates and bring earth's fair fruits
15   and lovely Peace and well-tressed Health;
and do banish disease and pain to mountain peaks.

37. TO THE TITANS,
incense - frankincense

Titans, glorious children of Ouranos and Gaia,
forbears of our fathers, who dwell down below
in Tartarean homes, in the earth's bowels.
From you stem all toiling mortals,
5   the creatures of the sea and of the land,
the birds,
and all generations of this world come from you,
and upon you I call to banish harsh anger,
if some earthly ancestor of mine stormed your
homes.

38. TO THE KOURETES,
incense - frankincense

Bronze-beating Kouretes, with Ares' armament,
dwellers of heaven, earth and sea, thrice-blessed,
life-giving breezes, glorious saviors of the world,
who dwell in the sacred land of Samothrace
5   and who ward off dangers for mortals roaming the
seas.
You were first to set up sacred rites for mortals,
O immortal Kouretes, with Ares' armament.
You rule Okeanos, and likewise you rule the sea
and the forests.
The earth resounds with the pounding of your
nimble feet,
10   as you come in your gleaming armor. All wild
beasts cringe
at your onrush, and the noise and shouts rise
heavenward,
while the dust from your briskly marching feet
reaches the clouds. Then every flower is in bloom.

δαίμονες ἀθάνατοι, τροφέες καὶ αὖτ᾽ ὀλετῆρες,
15 ἡνίκ᾽ ἂν ὁρμαίνητε χολούμενοι ἀνθρώποισιν
ὀλλύντες βίοτον καὶ κτήματα ἠδὲ καὶ αὐτοὺς
† πιμπλάντες, στοναχεῖ δὲ μέγας πόντος βαθυδίνης,
δένδρη δ᾽ ὑψικάρην᾽ ἐκ ῥιζῶν ἐς χθόνα πίπτει,
ἠχὼ δ᾽ οὐρανία κελαδεῖ ῥοιζήμασι φύλλων.
20 Κουρῆτες Κορύβαντες, ἀνάκτορες εὐδύνατοί τε
ἐν Σαμοθράικηι ἄνακτες, ὁμοῦ ⟨δὲ⟩ Διόσκοροι αὐτοί,
πνοιαὶ ἀέναοι, ψυχοτρόφοι, ἀεροειδεῖς,
οἵτε καὶ οὐράνιοι δίδυμοι κλήιζεσθ᾽ ἐν Ὀλύμπωι,
εὔπνοοι, εὔδιοι, σωτήριοι ἠδὲ προσηνεῖς,
25 ὡροτρόφοι, φερέκαρποι ἐπιπνείοιτε ἄνακτες.

39 Κορύβαντος, θυμίαμα λίβανον.

Κικλήσκω χθονὸς ἀενάου βασιλῆα μέγιστον,
Κύρβαντ᾽ ὀλβιόμοιρον, Ἀρήιον, ἀπροσόρατον,
νυκτερινὸν Κουρῆτα, φόβων ἀποπαύστορα δεινῶν,
φαντασιῶν ἐπαρωγόν, ἐρημοπλάνον Κορύβαντα,
5 αἰολόμορφον ἄνακτα, θεὸν διφυῆ, πολύμορφον,
φοίνιον, αἱμαχθέντα κασιγνήτων ὑπὸ δισσῶν,
Δηοῦς ὃς γνώμαισιν ἐνήλλαξας δέμας ἁγνόν,
θηρότυπον θέμενος μορφὴν δνοφεροῖο δράκοντος·
κλῦθι, μάκαρ, φωνῶν, χαλεπὴν δ᾽ ἀποπέμπεο μῆνιν,
10 παύων φαντασίας, ψυχῆς ἐκπλήκτου ἀνάγκας.

Immortal gods, you nurture, but you also destroy,
15   whenever angrily fretting over mankind,
you ruin livelihoods, possessions, and men them-
    selves.
... the great, deep-eddying sea groans,
lofty trees are uprooted and fall upon the earth,
and the tumult from the leaves echoes in the sky.
20   Kouretes - Korybantes, mighty lords,
masters of Samothrace, veritable Dioskouroi,
airy, soul-nourishing and ever-blowing breezes,
you are called celestial twins on Olympos.
As gentle saviors who bring fair breezes and clear
    weather,
25   and as nurturers of seasons and of fruits, breathe
    upon us, O lords!

39. TO KORYBAS,
incense - frankincense

I call upon the greatest king of eternal earth,
blessed Korybas, warlike, of forbidding counte-
    nance,
nocturnal Koures, who saves from dreadful fear.
Korybas, you assist the imagination and you wander
    in deserted places.
5   Lord, many are the shapes of your twofold divinity,
and the murder of the twin brothers has stained
    you with blood.
Following Deo's scheme, you changed your holy form
into the shape of a savage and dark dragon.
Blessed one, hear our voices, banish harsh anger,
10   and free from fantasies a soul stunned by
    necessity.

40 Δήμητρος Ἐλευσινίας, θυμίαμα στύρακα.

Δηώ, παμμήτειρα θεά, πολυώνυμε δαῖμον,
σεμνὴ Δήμητερ, κουροτρόφε, ὀλβιοδῶτι,
πλουτοδότειρα θεά, σταχυοτρόφε, παντοδότειρα,
εἰρήνηι χαίρουσα καὶ ἐργασίαις πολυμόχθοις,
5   σπερμεία, σωρῖτι, ἀλωαία, χλοόκαρπε,
ἢ ναίεις ἁγνοῖσιν Ἐλευσῖνος γυάλοισιν,
ἱμερόεσσ᾽, ἐρατή, θνητῶν θρέπτειρα προπάντων,
ἡ πρώτη ζεύξασα βοῶν ἀροτῆρα τένοντα
καὶ βίον ἱμερόεντα βροτοῖς πολύολβον ἀνεῖσα,
10   αὐξιθαλής, Βρομίοιο συνέστιος, ἀγλαότιμος,
λαμπαδόεσσ᾽, ἁγνή, δρεπάνοις χαίρουσα θερείοις·
σὺ χθονία, σὺ δὲ φαινομένη, σὺ δὲ πᾶσι προσηνής·
εὔτεκνε, παιδοφίλη, σεμνή, κουροτρόφε κούρα,
ἅρμα δρακοντείοισιν ὑποζεύξασα χαλινοῖς
15   ἐγκυκλίοις δίναις περὶ σὸν θρόνον εὐάζουσα,
μουνογενής, πολύτεκνε θεά, πολυπότνια θνητοῖς,
ἧς πολλαὶ μορφαί, πολυάνθεμοι, ἱεροθαλεῖς.
ἐλθέ, μάκαιρ᾽, ἁγνή, καρποῖς βρίθουσα θερείοις,
εἰρήνην κατάγουσα καὶ εὐνομίην ἐρατεινὴν
20   καὶ πλοῦτον πολύολβον, ὁμοῦ δ᾽ ὑγίειαν ἄνασσαν.

40. TO ELEUSINIAN DEMETER,
                    incense - storax

Deo, divine mother of all, goddess of many names,
august Demeter, nurturer of youths and giver of
    prosperity
and wealth. You nourish the ears of corn, O giver
    of all,
and you delight in peace and in toilsome labor.
5   Present at sowing, heaping and threshing, O spirit
    of the unripe fruit,
you dwell in the sacred valley of Eleusis.
Charming and lovely, you give sustenance to all
    mortals,
and you were the first to yoke the ploughing ox
and to send up from below a rich and lovely harvest
    for mortals.
10   Through you there is growth and blooming, O illus-
    trious companion of Bromios
and, torch-bearing and pure one, you delight in the
    summer's yield.
From beneath the earth you appear and to all you
    are gentle,
O holy and youth-nurturing lover of children and
    of fair offspring.
You yoke your chariot to bridled dragons,
15   and round your throne you whirl and howl in
    ecstasy.
Only daughter with many children and many powers
    over mortals,
you manifest your myriad faces to the variety of
    flowers and sacred blossoms;
come, blessed and pure one, and laden with the
    fruits of summer,
bring peace together with the welcome rule of law,
20   riches, too, and prosperity, and health that
    governs all.

41 Μητρὸς Ἀνταίας, θυμίαμα ἀρώματα.

Ἀνταία βασίλεια, θεά, πολυώνυμε μῆτερ
ἀθανάτων τε θεῶν ἠδὲ θνητῶν ἀνθρώπων,
ἥ ποτε μαστεύουσα πολυπλάγκτωι ἐν ἀνίηι
νηστείαν κατέπαυσας Ἐλευσῖνος {ἐν} γυάλοισιν
5   ἦλθές τ᾽ εἰς Ἀίδην πρὸς ἀγαυὴν Περσεφόνειαν
ἁγνὸν παῖδα Δυσαύλου ὁδηγητῆρα λαβοῦσα,
μηνυτῆρ᾽ ἁγίων λέκτρων χθονίου Διὸς ἁγνοῦ,
Εὔβουλον τέξασα θεὸν θνητῆς ὑπ᾽ ἀνάγκης.
ἀλλά, θεά, λίτομαί σε, πολυλλίστη βασίλεια,
10   ἐλθεῖν εὐάντητον ἐπ᾽ εὐιέρωι σέο μύστηι.

42 Μίσης, θυμίαμα στύρακα.

Θεσμοφόρον καλέω ναρθηκοφόρον Διόνυσον,
σπέρμα πολύμνηστον, πολυώνυμον Εὐβουλῆος,
ἁγνήν εὐίερόν τε Μίσην ἄρρητον ἄνασσαν,

ἄρσενα καὶ θῆλυν, διφυῆ, λύσειον Ἴακχον·
5   εἴτ᾽ ἐν Ἐλευσῖνος τέρπηι νηῶι θυόεντι,
εἴτε καὶ ἐν Φρυγίηι σὺν Μητέρι μυστιπολεύεις,
ἢ Κύπρωι τέρπηι σὺν ἐυστεφάνωι Κυθερείηι,
ἢ καὶ πυροφόροις πεδίοις ἐπαγάλλεαι ἁγνοῖς
σὺν σῆι μητρὶ θεᾶι μελανηφόρωι Ἴσιδι σεμνῆι,
10   Αἰγύπτου παρὰ χεῦμα σὺν ἀμφιπόλοισι τιθήναις·
εὐμενέουσ᾽ ἔλθοις ἀγαθοῖς † τελέουσ᾽ ἐπ᾽ ἀέθλοις.

41. TO MOTHER ANTAIA,
                    incense - aromatic herbs

Queen Antaia, goddess and many-named mother
of immortal gods and mortal men,
weary from searching and wandering far and wide,
you once ended your fast in the valley of Eleusis
5   and came to Hades for noble Persephone.
Your guide was the guileless child of Dysaules
who brought the news of pure chthonic Zeus' holy
        union.
Yielding to human need you bore divine Euboulos.
But, O goddess and queen to whom many pray, I
        beseech you
10   to come graciously to your pious initiate.

42. TO MISE,
                    incense - storax

I call upon law-giving Dionysos who carries the
        fennel stalk -
unforgettable and many-named seed of Eubouleus -
and upon holy, sacred and ineffable queen Mise,
whose twofold nature is male and female. As re-
        deeming Iacchos,
5   I summon you, lord, whether you delight in your
        fragrant temple at Eleusis,
or with the Mother you partake of mystic rites
        in Phrygia,
or you rejoice in Cyprus with fair-wreathed
        Kythereia,
or yet you exult in hallowed wheat-bearing fields
        along
Egypt's river with your divine mother,
10   the august and black-robed Isis, and your train
        of nurses.
Lady, kind-heartedly come to those contesting for
        noble prizes.

43 Ὡρῶν, θυμίαμα ἀρώματα.

Ὧραι θυγατέρες Θέμιδος καὶ Ζηνὸς ἄνακτος,
Εὐνομίη τε Δίκη τε καὶ Εἰρήνη πολύολβε,
εἰαριναί, λειμωνιάδες, πολυάνθεμοι, ἁγναί,
παντόχροοι, πολύοδμοι ἐν ἀνθεμοειδέσι πνοιαῖς,
5 Ὧραι ἀειθαλέες, περικυκλάδες, ἡδυπρόσωποι,
πέπλους ἐννύμεναι δροσεροὺς ἀνθῶν πολυθρέπτων,
⟨ἁγνῆς⟩ Περσεφόνης συμπαίκτορες, ἡνίκα Μοῖραι
καὶ Χάριτες κυκλίοισι χοροῖς πρὸς φῶς ἀνάγωσι
Ζηνὶ χαριζόμεναι καὶ μητέρι καρποδοτείρηι·
10 ἔλθετ᾽ ἐπ᾽ εὐφήμους τελετὰς ὁσίας νεομύστοις
εὐκάρπους καιρῶν γενέσεις ἐπάγουσαι ἀμεμφῶς.

44 Σεμέλης, θυμίαμα στύρακα.

Κικλήσκω κούρην Καδμηίδα παμβασίλειαν,
εὐειδῆ Σεμέλην, ἐρατοπλόκαμον, βαθύκολπον,
μητέρα θυρσοφόροιο Διωνύσου πολυγηθοῦς,
ἣ μεγάλας ὠδῖνας ἐλάσσατο πυρφόρωι αὐγῆι
5 ἀθανάτου φλεχθεῖσα Διὸς βουλαῖς Κρονίοιο
τιμὰς τευξαμένη παρ᾽ ἀγαυῆς Περσεφονείης
ἐν θνητοῖσι βροτοῖσιν ἀνὰ τριετηρίδας ὥρας,
ἡνίκα σοῦ Βάκχου γονίμην ὠδῖνα τελῶσιν
εὐίερόν τε τράπεζαν ἰδὲ μυστήριά θ᾽ ἁγνά.

43. TO THE HORAI,
incense - aromatic herbs

Horai, daughters of Themis and of Lord Zeus -
Eunomie and Dike and thrice-blessed Eirene -
pure spirits of spring and of the blossoming
    meadow,
you are found in every color and in all scents
    wafted by the breezes.
5   Ever-blooming, revolving and sweet-faced, O Horai,
you cloak yourselves with the dew of luxuriant
    flowers.
You are holy Persephone's companions at play,
    when the Fates
and the Graces, in circling dances come forth to
    light,
pleasing Zeus and their fruit-giving mother.
10   Come to the new initiates and their reverent and
    holy rites
and bring seasons perfect for the growth of
    goodly fruit.

44. TO SEMELE,
incense - storax

I call upon the daughter of Kadmos, queen of all,
fair Semele of the lovely tresses and the full
    bosom,
mother of thyrsus-bearing and joyous Dionysos.
She was driven to great pain by the blazing
    thunderbolt
5   which, through the counsels of immortal Kronian
    Zeus, burned her,
and by noble Persephone she was granted honors
among mortal men, honors given every third year.
Then they reenact the travail for your son Bacchos,
the sacred ritual of the table, and the holy
    mysteries.

10 νῦν σέ, θεά, λίτομαι, κούρη Καδμηίς, ἄνασσα,
πρηύνοον καλέων αἰεὶ μύσταισιν ὑπάρχειν.

45 Ὕμνος Διονύσου Βασσαρέως Τριετηρικοῦ.

Ἐλθέ, μάκαρ Διόνυσε, πυρίσπορε, ταυρομέτωπε,
Βάσσαρε καὶ Βακχεῦ, πολυώνυμε, παντοδυνάστα,
ὃς ξίφεσιν χαίρεις ἠδ' αἵματι Μαινάσι θ' ἁγναῖς,
εὐάζων κατ' Ὄλυμπον, ἐρίβρομε, † μανικὲ Βάκχε,
5 θυρσεγχής, βαρύμηνι, τετιμένε πᾶσι θεοῖσι
καὶ θνητοῖσι βροτοῖσιν, ὅσοι χθόνα ναιετάουσιν·
ἐλθέ, μάκαρ, σκιρτητά, φέρων πολὺ γῆθος ἅπασι.

46 Λικνίτου, θυμίαμα μάνναν.

Λικνίτην Διόνυσον ἐπ' εὐχαῖς ταῖσδε κικλήσκω,
Νύσιον ἀμφιθαλῆ, πεποθημένον, εὔφρονα Βάκχον,
νυμφῶν ἔρνος ἐραστὸν ἐυστεφάνου τ' Ἀφροδίτης.
ὅς ποτ' ἀνὰ δρυμοὺς κεχορευμένα βήματα πάλλες
5 σὺν νύμφαις χαρίεσσιν ἐλαυνόμενος μανίῃσι,
καὶ βουλαῖσι Διὸς πρὸς ἀγαυὴν Φερσεφόνειαν
ἀχθεὶς ἐξετράφης φίλος ἀθανάτοισι θεοῖσιν.
εὔφρων ἐλθέ, μάκαρ, κεχαρισμένα δ' ἱερὰ δέξαι.

10 Now you, goddess, do I beseech, daughter of Kadmos,
      queen,
    always to be gentle-minded toward the initiates.

45. HYMN TO DIONYSOS.
BASSAREUS AND TRIENNIAL

Come, blessed Dionysos, bull-faced god conceived
    in fire,
Bassareus and Bacchos, many-named master of all.
You delight in bloody swords and in the holy
    menads,
as you howl throughout Olympos, O roaring and
    frenzied Bacchos.
5 Armed with the thyrsus and wrathful in the extreme,
      you are honored   .
by all the gods and by all the men who dwell upon
    the earth.
Come, blessed and leaping god, and bring much joy
    to all.

46. TO LIKNITES,
incense - powdered frankincense

I summon to these prayers Dionysos Liknites,
born at Nysa, blossoming, beloved and kindly
    Bacchos,
nursling of the nymphs and of fair-wreathed
    Aphrodite.
the forests once felt your feet quiver in the
    dance
5 as frenzy drove you and the graceful nymphs on
      and on,
and the counsels of Zeus brought you to noble
    Persephone
who reared you to be loved by the deathless gods.
Kind-heartedly come, O blessed one, and accept
    the gift of this sacrifice.

47 Περικιονίου, θυμίαμα ἀρώματα.

Κικλήσκω Βάκχον περικιόνιον, μεθυδώτην,
Καδμείοισι δόμοις ὃς ἑλισσόμενος πέρι πάντη
ἔστησε κρατερῶς βρασμοὺς γαίης ἀποπέμψας,
ἡνίκα πυρφόρος αὐγὴ ἐκίνησε χθόνα πᾶσαν
5   πρηστῆρος ῥοίζοις· ὃ δ' ἀνέδραμε δεσμὸς ἁπάντων.
ἐλθέ, μάκαρ, βακχευτά, γεγηθυίαις πραπίδεσσιν.

48 Σαβαζίου, θυμίαμα ἀρώματα.

Κλῦθι, πάτερ, Κρόνου υἱέ, Σαβάζιε, κύδιμε δαῖμον,
ὃς Βάκχον Διόνυσον, ἐρίβρομον, εἰραφιώτην,
μηρῶι ἐγκατέραψας, ὅπως τετελεσμένος ἔλθηι
Τμῶλον ἐς ἡγάθεον παρ⟨ὰ⟩ Ἵπταν καλλιπάρηιον.
5   ἀλλά, μάκαρ, Φρυγίης μεδέων, βασιλεύτατε πάντων,
εὐμενέων ἐπαρωγὸς ἐπέλθοις μυστιπόλοισιν.

49 Ἵπτας, θυμίαμα στύρακα.

Ἵπταν κικλήσκω, Βάκχου τροφόν, εὐάδα κούρην,
μυστιπόλον, τελεταῖσιν ἀγαλλομένην Σάβου ἁγνοῦ
νυκτερίοις τε χοροῖσιν ἐριβρεμέταο Ἰάκχου.
κλῦθί μου εὐχομένου, χθονία μήτηρ, βασίλεια,
5   εἴτε σύ γ' ἐν Φρυγίηι κατέχεις Ἴδης ὄρος ἁγνὸν
ἢ Τμῶλος τέρπει σε, καλὸν Λυδοῖσι θόασμα·
ἔρχεο πρὸς τελετὰς ἱερῶι γήθουσα προσώπωι.

47. TO PERIKIONIOS,
incense - aromatic herbs

I call upon Bacchos Perikionios, giver of wine,
who enveloped all of Kadmos' house
and with his might checked and calmed the heaving
   earth
when the blazing thunderbolt and the raging gale
5   stirred all the land. Then everyone's bonds
   sprang loose.
Blessed reveler, come with joyful heart.

48. TO SABAZIOS,
incense - aromatic herbs

Hear me, father Sabazios, son of Kronos, illustrious god.
You sewed into your thigh Bacchic Dionysos,
   the roaring
Eiraphiotes, that he might come whole
to noble Tmolos, by the side of fair-cheeked
   Hipta.
5   But, O blessed ruler of Phrygia and supreme king
   of all,
come kind-heartedly to the aid of the initiates.

49. TO HIPTA,
incense - storax

I call upon Hipta, nurse of Bacchos, maiden
   possessed.
In mystic rites she takes part, and she exults in
   pure Sabos' worship
and in the night dances of roaring Iacchos.
O queen and chthonic mother, hear my prayer,
5   whether you are on Ida, Phrygia's sacred mountain,
or you take your pleasure on Tmolos, fair seat of
   the Lydians.
Come to these rites, with joy on your holy face.

50 Λυσίου Ληναίου.

Κλῦθι, μάκαρ, Διὸς υἷ’, ἐπιλήνιε Βάκχε, διμάτωρ,
σπέρμα πολύμνη⟨σ⟩τον, πολυώνυμε, λύσιε δαῖμον,
κρυψίγονον μακάρων ἱερὸν θάλος, εὔιε Βάκχε,
εὐτραφές, εὔκαρπε, πολυγηθέα καρπὸν ἀέξων,
ῥηξίχθων, ληναῖε, μεγασθενές, αἰολόμορφε,
παυσίπονον θνητοῖσι φανεὶς ἄκος, ἱερὸν ἄνθος,
χάρμα βροτοῖς φιλάλυπον, † ἐπάφιε, καλλιέθειρε,
λύσιε, θυρσομανές, βρόμι’, εὔιε, πᾶσιν ἐύφρων,
οἷς ἐθέλεις θνητῶν ἠδ’ ἀθανάτων † ἐπιφαύσκων
νῦν σε καλῶ μύσταισι μολεῖν ἡδύν, φερέκαρπον.

51 Νυμφῶν, θυμίαμα ἀρώματα.

Νύμφαι, θυγατέρες μεγαλήτορος Ὠκεανοῖο,
ὑγροπόροις γαίης ὑπὸ κεύθεσιν οἰκί’ ἔχουσαι,
κρυψίδρομοι, Βάκχοιο τροφοί, χθόνιαι, πολυγηθεῖς,
καρποτρόφοι, λειμωνιάδες, σκολιοδρόμοι, ἁγναί,
ἀντροχαρεῖς, σπήλυγξι κεχαρμέναι, ἠερόφοιτοι,
πηγαῖαι, δρομάδες, δροσοείμονες, ἴχνεσι κοῦφαι,
φαινόμεναι, ἀφανεῖς, αὐλωνιάδες, πολυανθεῖς,
σὺν Πανὶ σκιρτῶσαι ἀν’ οὔρεα, εὐάστειραι,

50. TO LYSIOS - LENAIOS

Hear, O blessed son of Zeus and of two mothers,
   Bacchos of the vintage,
unforgettable seed, many-named and redeeming demon,
holy offspring of the gods born in secrecy,
   reveling Bacchos,
plump giver of the many joys of fruits which grow
   well.
5   Mighty and many-shaped god, from the earth you
   burst forth to reach the wine-press
and there become a remedy for man's pain,
   O sacred blossom!
A sorrow-hating joy to mortals, O lovely-haired
   Epaphian,
you are a redeemer and a reveler whose thyrsus
   drives to frenzy
and who is kind-hearted to all, gods and mortals,
   who see his light.
10   I call upon you now to come, a sweet bringer of
   fruit.

51. TO THE NYMPHS,
incense - aromatic herbs

Nymphs, daughters of great-hearted Okeanos,
you dwell inside the earth's damp caves
and your paths are secret, O joyous and chthonic
   ones, nurses of Bacchos.
You nourish fruits and haunt meadows, O sprightly
   and pure
5   travelers of the winding roads who delight in
   caves and grottoes.
Swift, light-footed, and clothed in dew, you
   frequent springs;
visible and invisible, in ravines and among
   flowers,
you shout and frisk with Pan upon mountain sides.

πετρόρυτοι, λιγυραί, βομβήτριαι, οὐρεσίφοιτοι,
10 ἀγρότεραι κοῦραι, κρουνίτιδες ὑλονόμοι τε,
παρϑένοι εὐώδεις, λευχείμονες, εὔπνοοι αὔραις,
αἰπολικαί, νόμιαι, ϑηρσὶν φίλαι, ἀγλαόκαρποι,
κρυμοχαρεῖς, ἁπαλαί, πολυϑρέμμονες αὐξίτροφοί τε,
κοῦραι ἁμαδρυάδες, φιλοπαίγμονες, ὑγροκέλευϑοι,
15 Νύσιαι, † μανικαί, παιωνίδες, εἰαροτερπεῖς,
σὺν Βάκχωι Δηοῖ τε χάριν ϑνητοῖσι φέρουσαι·
ἔλϑετ᾿ ἐπ᾿ εὐφήμοις ἱεροῖς κεχαρηότι ϑυμῶι
νᾶμα χέουσαι ὑγεινὸν ἀεξιτρόφοισιν ἐν ὥραις.

52 Τριετηρικοῦ, ϑυμίαμα ἀρώματα.

Κικλήσκω σε, μάκαρ, πολυώνυμε, † μανικέ, Βακχεῦ,
ταυρόκερως, ληναῖε, πυρίσπορε, Νύσιε, λυσεῦ,
μηροτρεφής, λικνῖτα, † πυριπόλε καὶ τελετάρχα,
νυκτέρι᾿, Εὐβουλεῦ, μιτρηφόρε, ϑυρσοτινάκτα,
5 ὄργιον ἄρρητον, τριφυές, κρύφιον Διὸς ἔρνος,
πρωτόγον᾿, Ἠρικεπαῖε, ϑεῶν πάτερ ἠδὲ καὶ υἱέ,
ὠμάδιε, σκηπτοῦχε, χοροιμανές, ἀγέτα κώμων,
βακχεύων ἁγίας τριετηρίδας ἀμφὶ γαληνάς,

Gliding down on rocks, you hum with clear voice,
O mountain-haunting
10   sylvan maidens of the fields and streams.
O sweet-smelling virgins, clad in white, fresh
as the breezes,
with goatherds, pastures and splendid fruits in
your domain. You are loved by creatures of
the wild.
Tender though you are, you rejoice in cold and you
give sustenance and growth to many,
O playful and water-loving Hamadryad maidens.
15   Dwellers of Nysa, frenzied and healing goddesses
who joy in spring,
together with Bacchos and Deo you bring grace to
mortals.
With joyful hearts come to this hallowed sacrifice
and in the seasons of growth pour streams of
salubrious rain.

52. TO THE GOD OF TRIENNIAL FEASTS,
incense - aromatic herbs

I call upon you, blessed, many-named and frenzied
Bacchos,
bull-horned Nysian redeemer, god of the wine-press,
conceived in fire.
Nourished in the thigh, O Lord of the Cradle, you
marshal torch-lit processions
in the night, O filleted and thyrsus-shaking
Eubouleus.
5   Threefold is your nature and ineffable your rites,
O secret offspring of Zeus;
primeval, Erikepaios, father and son of gods,
you take raw flesh and, sceptered, you lead into
the madness of revel and dance
in the frenzy of triennial feasts that bestow
calm on us.

10 ῥηξίχθων, πυριφεγγές, † ἐπάφριε, κοῦρε διμάτωρ,
ούρεσιφοῖτα, κερώς, νεβριδοστόλε, ἀμφιέτηρε,
Παιὰν χρυσεγχής, † ὑποκόλπιε, βοτρυόκοσμε,
Βάσσαρε, κισσοχαρής, † πολυπάρθενε καὶ διάκοσμε †
ἐλθέ, μάκαρ, μύσταισι βρύων κεχαρημένος αἰεί.

53 Ἀμφιετοῦς, θυμίαμα πάντα πλὴν λιβάνου καὶ σπένδε γάλα.
Ἀμφιετῆ καλέω Βάκχον, χθόνιον Διόνυσον,
ἐγρόμενον κούραις ἅμα νύμφαις εὐπλοκάμοισ⟨ιν⟩,
ὃς παρὰ Περσεφόνης ἱεροῖσι δόμοισιν ἰαύων
κοιμίζει τριετῆρα χρόνον, Βακχήιον ἁγνόν.
5 αὐτὸς δ᾽ ἡνίκα τὸν τριετῆ πάλι κῶμον ἐγείρηι,
εἰς ὕμνον τρέπεται σὺν ἐυζώνοισι τιθήναις
εὐνάζων κινῶν τε χρόνους ἐνὶ κυκλάσιν ὥραις.
ἀλλά, μάκαρ, χλοόκαρπε, κερασφόρε, κάρπιμε Βάκχε,
βαῖν᾽ ἐπὶ πάνθειον τελετὴν γανόωντι προσώπωι
10 εὐιέροις καρποῖσι τελεσσιγόνοισι βρυάζων.

You burst forth from the earth in a blaze ...,
   O son of two mothers,
10   and, horned and clad in fawnskin, you roam the
   mountains, O lord worshiped in annual feasts.
Paian of the golden spear, nursling, decked with
   grapes,
Bassaros, exulting in ivy, followed by many
   maidens....
Joyous and all-abounding, come, O blessed one,
   to the initiates.

53.   TO THE GOD OF ANNUAL FEASTS,
      incense - all other things save frankin-
      cense -- a libation of milk, too.

I call upon the Bacchos we worship annually,
   chthonic Dionysos
who, together with the fair-tressed nymphs, is
   roused.
In the sacred halls of Persephone he slumbers
and puts to sleep pure, Bacchic time every third
   year.
5   When he himself stirs up the triennial revel again
he sings a hymn, accompanied by his fair-girdled
   nurses,
and, as the seasons revolve, he puts to sleep and
   wakes up the years.
But, O blessed and fruit-giving Bacchos, O horned
   spirit of the unripe fruit,
come to this most sacred rite with the glow of joy
   on your face,
10   come all-abounding in fruit that is holy and
   perfect.

54 Σιληνοῦ Σατύρου Βακχῶν, θυμίαμα μάνναν.

Κλῦθί μου, ὦ πολύσεμνε τροφεῦ, Βάκχοιο τιθηνέ,
Σιληνῶν ὄχ' ἄριστε, τετιμένε πᾶσι θεοῖσι
καὶ θνητοῖσι βροτοῖσιν ἐπὶ τριετηρίσιν ὥραις,
ἁγνοτελής, γεραρός, θιάσου νομίου τελετάρχα,
5   εὐαστής, φιλάγρυπνε σὺν εὐζώνοισι τιθήναις,
Ναῖσι καὶ Βάκχαις ἡγούμενε κισσοφόροισι·
δεῦρ' ἐπὶ πάνθειον τελετὴν Σατύροις ἅμα πᾶσι
θηροτύποις, εὔασμα διδοὺς Βακχείου ἄνακτος,
σὺν Βάκχαις Λήναια τελεσφόρα σεμνὰ προπέμπων,
10   ὄργια νυκτιφαῆ τελεταῖς ἁγίαις ἀναφαίνων,
εὐάζων, φιλόθυρσε, γαληνιόων θιάσοισιν.

55 Εἰς Ἀφροδίτην.

Οὐρανία, πολύυμνε, φιλομμειδὴς Ἀφροδίτη,
ποντογενής, γενέτειρα θεά, φιλοπάννυχε, σεμνή,
νυκτερία Ζεύκτειρα, δολοπλόκε μῆτερ Ἀνάγκης·
πάντα γὰρ ἐκ σέθεν ἐστίν, ὑπεζεύξω δέ ⟨τε⟩ κόσμον
5   καὶ κρατέεις τρισσῶν μοιρῶν, γεννᾷς δὲ τὰ πάντα,
ὅσσα τ' ἐν οὐρανῶι ἐστι καὶ ἐν γαίηι πολυκάρπωι
ἐν πόντου τε βυθῶι {τε}, σεμνὴ Βάκχοιο πάρεδρε,
τερπομένη θαλίαισι, γαμοστόλε μῆτερ Ἐρώτων,
Πειθοῖ λεκτροχαρής, κρυφία, χαριδῶτι,
10   φαινομένη, {τ'}ἀφανής, ἐρατοπλόκαμ', εὐπατέρεια,

54. TO SILENOS, SATYROS, AND THE BACCHAI,
incense - powdered frankincense

Hear me Bacchos' foster father and nurturer,
by far best of the Silenoi, honored by all the
  gods
and by mortal men in the same triennial feasts.
Pure and honored marshal of the pastoral band,
5   wakeful reveler and companion of the fair-girt
  nurses,
leader of the ivy-crowned Naiads and Bacchantes,
take all the Satyrs - half men and half beasts -
and come howling to the Bacchic lord.
With the Bacchantes escort the holy Lenean pro-
  cession,
10   in sacred litanies revealing torch-lit rites,
shouting, thyrsus-loving, finding calm in the
  revels.

55. TO APHRODITE

Heavenly, smiling Aphrodite, praised in many hymns,
sea-born, revered goddess of generation, you like
  the nightlong revel
and you couple lovers at night, O scheming mother
  of Necessity.
Everything comes from you; you have yoked the
  world,
5   and you control all three realms. You give birth
  to all,
to everything in heaven, upon the fruitful earth
and in the depths of the sea, O venerable companion of Bacchos.
You delight in festivities, O bridelike mother of
  the Erotes,
O Persuasion whose joy is in the bed of love,
  secretive, giver of grace,
10   visible and invisible, lovely-tressed daughter of
  a noble father,

νυμφιδία σύνδαιτι θεῶν, σκηπτοῦχε, λύκαινα,
γεννοδότειρα, φίλανδρε, ποθεινοτάτη, βιοδῶτι,
ἡ ζεύξασα βροτοὺς ἀχαλινώτοισιν ἀνάγκαις
καὶ θηρῶν πολὺ φῦλον ἐρωτομανῶν ὑπὸ φίλτρων·
15 ἔρχεο, Κυπρογενὲς θεῖον γένος, εἴτ᾽ ἐν᾽ Ὀλύμπωι
ἐσσί, θεὰ βασίλεια, καλῶι γήθουσα προσώπωι,
εἴτε καὶ εὐλιβάνου Συρίης ἕδος ἀμφιπολεύεις,
εἴτε σύ γ᾽ ἐν πεδίοισι σὺν ἅρμασι χρυσεοτεύκτοις
Αἰγύπτου κατέχεις ἱερῆς γονιμώδεα λουτρά,
20 ἢ καὶ κυκνείοισιν ὄχοις ἐπὶ πόντιον οἶδμα
ἐρχομένη χαίρεις κητῶν κυκλίαισι χορείαις,
ἢ νύμφαις τέρπηι κυανώπισιν ἐν χθονὶ δίηι
† θῖνας ἐπ᾽ αἰγιαλοῖς ψαμμώδεσιν ἅλματι κούφωι·
εἴτ᾽ ἐν Κύπρωι, ἄνασσα, τροφῶι σέο, ἔνθα καλαί σε
25 παρθένοι ἄδμηται νύμφαι τ᾽ ἀνὰ πάντ᾽ ἐνιαυτὸν
ὑμνοῦσιν, σέ, μάκαιρα, καὶ ἄμβροτον ἁγνὸν Ἄδωνιν.
ἐλθέ, μάκαιρα θεά μάλ᾽ ἐπήρατον εἶδος ἔχουσα·
ψυχῆι γάρ σε καλῶ σεμνῆι ἁγίοισι λόγοισιν.

56 Ἀδώνιδος, θυμίαμα ἀρώματα.

Κλῦθί μου εὐχομένου, πολυώνυμε, δαῖμον ἄριστε,
ἁβροκόμη, φιλέρημε, βρύων ὠιδαῖσι ποθειναῖς,
Εὐβουλεῦ, πολύμορφε, τροφεῦ πάντων ἀρίδηλε,
κούρη καὶ κόρε, † σὺ πᾶσιν † θάλος αἰέν, Ἄδωνι,
5 σβεννύμενε λάμπων τε καλαῖς ἐν κυκλάσιν ὥραις,

bridal feast companion of the gods, sceptered
   she-wolf,
beloved and man-loving giver of birth and of life,
with your maddening love-charms you yoke mortals
and the many races of beasts to unbridled passion.
15   Come, O goddess born in Cyprus, whether you are on
   Olympos,
O queen, exulting in the beauty of your face,
or you wander in Syria, country of fine frankincense,
or, yet, driving your golden chariot in the plain,
you lord it over Egypt's fertile river bed.
20   Come, whether you ride your swan-drawn chariot
   over the sea's billows,
joying in the creatures of the deep as they dance
   in circles,
or you delight in the company of the dark-faced
   nymphs on land,
(as, light-footed, they frisk over the sandy
   beaches).
Come, lady, even if you are in Cyprus that
   cherishes you,
25   where fair maidens and chaste nymphs throughout
   the year
sing of you, O blessed one, and of immortal,
   pure Adonis.
Come, O beautiful and comely goddess;
I summon you with holy words and pious soul.

56. TO ADONIS,
incense - aromatic herbs

Hear my prayer, O best and many-named god.
Fine-haired, solitary and full of lovely song;
Eubouleus, many-shaped and noble nurturer of all,
maiden and youth in one, ... unwithering bloom,
   O Adonis,
5   you vanish and shine again in the fair seasons'
   turn.

αὐξιθαλής, δίκερως, πολυήρατε, δακρυότιμε,
ἀγλαόμορφε, κυναγεσίοις χαίρων, βαθυχαῖτα,
ἱμερόνους, Κύπριδος γλυκερὸν θάλος, ἔρνος Ἔρωτος,
Φερσεφόνης ἐρασιπλοκάμου λέκτροισι λοχευθείς,
10 ὃς ποτὲ μὲν ναίεις ὑπὸ Τάρταρον ἠερόεντα,
ἠδὲ πάλιν πρὸς Ὄλυμπον ἄγεις δέμας ὡριόκαρπον·
ἐλθέ, μάκαρ, μύσταισι φέρων καρποὺς ἀπὸ γαίης.

57 Ἑρμοῦ Χθονίου, θυμίαμα στύρακα.

Κωκυτοῦ ναίων ἀνυπόστροφον οἶμον ἀνάγκης,
ὃς ψυχὰς θνητῶν κατάγεις ὑπὸ νέρτερα γαίης,
Ἑρμῆ, βακχεχόροιο Διωνύσοιο γένεθλον
καὶ Παφίης κούρης, ἑλικοβλεφάρου Ἀφροδίτης,
5 ὃς παρὰ Περσεφόνης ἱερὸν δόμον ἀμφιπολεύεις,
αἰνομόροις ψυχαῖς πομπὸς κατὰ γαῖαν ὑπάρχων,
ἃς κατάγεις, ὁπόταν μοίρης χρόνος εἰσαφίκηται
εὐιέρωι ῥάβδωι θέλγων † ὑπνοδώτειρα πάντα,
καὶ πάλιν ὑπνώοντας ἐγείρεις· σοὶ γὰρ ἔδωκε {τιμὴν}
10 τιμὴν Φερσεφόνεια θεὰ κατὰ Τάρταρον εὐρὺν
ψυχαῖς ἀενάοις θνητῶν ὁδὸν ἡγεμονεύειν.
ἀλλά, μάκαρ, πέμποις μύσταις τέλος ἐσθλὸν ἐπ' ἔργοις.

Two-horned spirit of growth and blooming, much
    loved and wept for
you are, O fair and joyful hunter of the luxuri-
    ant mane.
Desire is in your mind, O sweet blossom and off-
    shoot of Aphrodite and Eros,
child born on the bed of lovely-tressed Persephone.
10   Now you dwell beneath murky Tartaros
and now again toward Olympos you bring your full-
    grown body.
Come, O blessed one, and bring earth's fruits to
    the initiates.

57. TO CHTHONIC HERMES,
incense - storax

You dwell in the compelling road of no return, by
    the Kokytos,
and you guide the souls of mortals to the nether
    gloom.
Hermes, offspring of Dionysos who revels in the
    dance
and of Aphrodite, the Paphian maiden of the flut-
    tering eyelids,
5   you frequent the sacred house of Persephone
as guide throughout the earth of ill-fated souls
which you bring to their haven when their time has
    come,
charming them with your sacred wand and giving
    them sleep
from which you rouse them again. To you indeed
10   Persephone gave the office, throughout wide
    Tartaros,
to lead the way for the eternal souls of men.
But, blessed one, grant a good end for the
    initiate's work.

58 Ἔρωτος, θυμίαμα ἀρώματα.

Κικλήσκω μέγαν, ἀγνόν, ἐράσμιον, ἡδὺν Ἔρωτα,
τοξαλκή, πτερόεντα, πυρίδρομον, εὔδρομον ὁρμῆι,
συμπαίζοντα θεοῖς ἠδὲ θνητοῖς ἀνθρώποις,
εὐπάλαμον, διφυῆ, πάντων κληῖδας ἔχοντα,
5   αἰθέρος οὐρανίου, πόντου, χθονός, ἠδ' ὅσα θνητοῖς
πνεύματα παντογένεθλα θεὰ βόσκει χλοόκαρπος,
ἠδ' ὅσα Τάρταρος εὐρὺς ἔχει πόντος· θ' ἀλίδουπος·
μοῦνος γὰρ τούτων πάντων οἴηκα κρατύνεις.
ἀλλά, μάκαρ, καθαραῖς γνώμαις μύσταισι συνέρχου,
10   φαύλους δ' ἐκτοπίους θ' ὁρμὰς ἀπὸ τῶνδ' ἀπόπεμπε.

59 Μοιρῶν, θυμίαμα ἀρώματα.

Μοῖραι ἀπειρέσιοι, Νυκτὸς φίλα τέκνα μελαίνης,
κλῦτέ μου εὐχομένου, πολυώνυμοι, αἵτ' ἐπὶ λίμνης
οὐρανίας, ἵνα λευκὸν ὕδωρ νυχίας ὑπὸ θέρμης
ῥήγνυται ἐν σκιερῶι λιπαρῶι μυχῶι εὐλίθου ἄντρου,
5   ναίουσαι πεπότησθε βροτῶν ἐπ' ἀπείρονα γαῖαν·
ἔνθεν ἐπὶ βρότεον δόκιμον γένος ἐλπίδι κοῦφον
στείχετε πορφυρέηισι καλυψάμεναι ὀθόνηισι
μορσίμωι ἐν πεδίωι, ὅθι πάγγεον ἄρμα διώκει
δόξα δίκης παρὰ τέρμα καὶ ἐλπίδος ἠδὲ μεριμνῶν
10   καὶ νόμου ὠγυγίου καὶ ἀπείρονος εὐνόμου ἀρχῆς·

58. TO EROS,
incense - aromatic herbs

I call upon great, pure, lovely and sweet Eros,
winged archer who runs swiftly on a path of fire
and plays together with gods and mortal men.
Inventive and two-natured, he is master of all,
5   of the heavenly ether, of the sea, of the land,
    of the all-begetting
winds which for mortals are nurtured by the goddess
    of the green fruit,
and of all that lies in Tartaros and in the
    roaring sea.
You alone govern the course of all these.
But, blessed one, come to the initiates, with pure
    thought,
10   and banish from them vile impulses.

59. TO THE FATES,
incense - aromatic herbs

Boundless Fates, dear children of dark night,
hear my prayer, O many-named dwellers on the lake
of heaven where the frozen water by night's warmth
is broken inside a sleek cave's shady hollow;
5   from there you fly to the boundless earth, home of
    mortals,
and thence, cloaked in purple, you march toward
    men
whose aims are as noble as their hopes are vain,
in the vale of doom, where glory drives her chariot
    on
all over the earth, beyond the goal of justice, of
    anxious hope,
10   of primeval law, and of the immeasurable principle
    of order.

Μοῖρα γὰρ ἐν βιότωι καθορᾶι μόνη, οὐδέ τις ἄλλος
ἀθανάτων, οἳ ἔχουσι κάρη νιφόεντος Ὀλύμπου,
καὶ Διὸς ὄμμα τέλειον· ἐπεί γ᾽ ὅσα γίγνεται ἡμῖν,
Μοῖρά τε καὶ Διὸς οἶδε νόος διὰ παντὸς ἅπαντα.
15 ἀλλά μοι εὐκταῖαι, μαλακόφρονες, ἠπιόθυμοι,
Ἄτροπε καὶ Λάχεσι, Κλωθώ, μόλετ᾽, εὐπατέρειαι,
ἀέριοι, ἀφανεῖς, ἀμετάτροποι, αἰὲν ἀτειρεῖς,
παντοδότειραι, ἀφαιρέτιδες, θνητοῖσιν ἀνάγκη·
Μοῖραι, ἀκούσατ᾽ ἐμῶν ὁσίων λοιβῶν τε καὶ εὐχῶν,
20 ἐρχόμεναι μύσταις λυσιπήμονες εὔφρονι βουλῆι.
{Μοιράων τέλος ἔλλαβ᾽ ἀοιδή, ἥν ὕφαν᾽ Ὀρφεύς}

60 Χαρίτων, θυμίαμα στύρακα.

Κλῦτέ μοι, ὦ Χάριτες μεγαλώνυμοι, ἀγλαότιμοι,
θυγατέρες Ζηνός τε καὶ Εὐνομίης βαθυκόλπου,
Ἀγλαΐη Θαλίη τε καὶ Εὐφροσύνη πολύολβε,
χαρμοσύνης γενέτειραι, ἐράσμιαι, εὔφρονες, ἁγναί,
5 αἰολόμορφοι, ἀειθαλέες, θνητοῖσι ποθειναί·
εὐκταῖαι, κυκλάδες, καλυκώπιδες, ἱμερόεσσαι·
ἔλθοιτ᾽ ὀλβοδότειραι, ἀεὶ μύσταισι προσηνεῖς.

61 Νεμέσεως ὕμνος.

Ὦ Νέμεσι, κλήιζω σε, θεά, βασίλεια μεγίστη,
πανδερκής, ἐσορῶσα βίον θνητῶν πολυφύλων·
ἀιδία, πολύσεμνε, μόνη χαίρουσα δικαίοις,
ἀλλάσσουσα λόγον πολυποίκιλον, ἄστατον αἰεί,

In life Fate alone watches; the other immortals
who dwell on the peaks of snowy Olympos do not,
except for Zeus' perfect eye. But Fate and Zeus'
 mind
know all things for all time.
15 I pray to you to come, gently and kindly,
Atropos, Lachesis, and Klotho, scions of noble
 stock.
Airy, invisible, inexorable, and ever
 indestructible,
you give all and take all, being to men the same
 as necessity.
Fates, hear my prayers and receive my libations,
20 gently coming to the initiates to free them from
 pain.
(This is the end of the Fates' song, which
 Orpheus composed.)

60. TO THE GRACES,
incense - storax

Hear me, O illustrious and renowned Graces,
daughters of Zeus and full-bosomed Eunomia,
Aglaia, Thalia, and blessed Euphrosyne,
lovely, wise and pure mothers of joy,
5 many-shaped, ever-blooming, beloved of mortals.
We pray that each in her turn, spellbinding and
 with petal-soft face,
come, ever accessible to the initiates, to confer
 prosperity.

61. HYMN TO NEMESIS

Nemesis, I call upon you, goddess and greatest
 queen,
whose all-seeing eye looks upon the lives of man's
 many races.
Eternal and revered, you alone rejoice in the just,
and you change and vary and shift your word.

82

5 ἣν πάντες δεδίασι βροτοὶ ζυγὸν αὐχένι θέντες·
σοὶ γὰρ ἀεὶ γνώμη πάντων μέλει, οὐδέ σε λήθει
ψυχὴ ὑπερφρονέουσα λόγων ἀδιακρίτωι ὁρμῆι.
πάντ' ἐσορᾷς καὶ πάντ' ἐπακούεις, {καὶ} πάντα βραβεύεις·
ἐν σοὶ δ' εἰσὶ δίκαι θνητῶν, πανυπέρτατε δαῖμον.
10 ἐλθέ, μάκαιρ', ἁγνή, μύσταις ἐπιτάρροθος αἰεί·
δὸς δ' ἀγαθὴν διάνοιαν ἔχειν, παύουσα πανεχθεῖς
γνώμας οὐχ ὁσίας, πανυπέρφρονας, ἀλλοπροσάλλας.

62 Δίκης, θυμίαμα λίβανον.

Ὄμμα Δίκης μέλπω πανδερκέος, ἀγλαομόρφου,
ἣ καὶ Ζηνὸς ἄνακτος ἐπὶ θρόνον ἱερὸν ἵζει
οὐρανόθεν καθορῶσα βίον θνητῶν πολυφύλων,
τοῖς ἀδίκοις τιμωρὸς ἐπιβρίθουσα δικαία,
5 ἐξ ἰσότητος ἀληθείαι συνάγουσ' ἀνόμοια·
πάντα γάρ, ὅσσα κακαῖς γνώμαις θνητοῖσιν ὀχεῖται
δύσκριτα, βουλομένοις τὸ πλέον βουλαῖς ἀδίκοισι,
μούνη ἐπεμβαίνουσα δίκην ἀδίκοις ἐπεγείρεις·
ἐχθρὰ τῶν ἀδίκων, εὔφρων δὲ σύνεσσι δικαίοις.
10 ἀλλά, θεά, μόλ' ἐπὶ γνώμαις ἐσθλαῖσι δικαία,
ὡς ἂν ἀεὶ βιοτῆς τὸ πεπρωμένον ἦμαρ ἐπέλθοι.

63 Δικαιοσύνης, θυμίαμα λίβανον.
Ὦ θνητοῖσι δικαιοτάτη, πολύολβε, ποθεινή,
ἐξ ἰσότητος ἀεὶ θνητοῖς χαίρουσα δικαίοις,

5   All who bear the yoke of mortality fear you,
for you care about the thoughts of all, and the
    soul
that vaunts foolishly and without discretion does
    not escape you.
You see all, you hear all, and all you arbitrate,
O sublime deity in whom resides justice for men.
10   Come, blessed and pure one, ever helpful to
    initiates,
and grant nobility of mind, putting an end to
    loathesome,
unholy thoughts, such as are fickle and haughty.

62. TO DIKE,
incense - frankincense

I sing of the all-seeing eye of comely and radiant
    Dike,
who sits upon the sacred throne of lord Zeus.
From heaven you look down on the lives of the many
    human races,
and crush the unjust with just retribution,
5   matching things disparate with fairness and truth.
For whenever base men consider matters that cannot
    be put
to trial easily, unjustly wishing more than is
    fair,
you intervene and rouse justice against the unjust.
An enemy to the unjust, you are a gentle companion
    of the just.
10   But, goddess, come in justice for thoughts that
    are noble
until that fated day on my life descends.

63. TO JUSTICE,
incense - frankincense

O paragon of justice to mortals, blessed and
    beloved one,
you take equal pleasure in all just men.

πάντιμ᾽, ὀλβιόμοιρε, Δικαιοσύνη μεγαλαυχής,
ἡ καθαραῖς γνώμαισ⟨ιν⟩ ἀεὶ τὰ δέοντα βραβεύεις,
ἄθραυστος το συνειδός· ἀεὶ θραύεις γὰρ ἅπαντας,
ὅσσοι μὴ τὸ σὸν ἦλθον ὑπὸ Ζυγόν, †ἀλλ᾽ ὑπὲρ αὐτοῦ†
πλάστιγξι βριαραῖσι παρεγκλίναντες ἀπλήστως·
ἀστασία⟨σ⟩τε, φίλη πάντων, φιλόκωμ᾽, ἐρατεινή,
εἰρήνηι χαίρουσα, βίον Ζηλοῦσα βέβαιον·
αἰεὶ γὰρ τὸ πλέον στυγέεις, ἰσότητι δὲ χαίρεις·
ἐν σοὶ γὰρ σοφίη ἀρετῆς τέλος ἐσθλὸν ἱκάνει.
κλῦθι, θεά, κακίην θνητῶν θραύουσα δικαίως,
ὡς ἂν ἰσορροπίαισιν ἀεὶ βίος ἐσθλὸς ὁδεύοι
θνητῶν ἀνθρώπων, οἳ ἀρούρης καρπὸν ἔδουσι,
καὶ Ζώιων πάντων, ὁπόσ᾽ ἐν κόλποισι τιθηνεῖ
γαῖα θεὰ μήτηρ καὶ πόντιος εἰνάλιος Ζεύς.

64 Ὕμνος Νόμου.

Ἀθανάτων καλέω καὶ θνητῶν ἁγνὸν ἄνακτα,
οὐράνιον Νόμον, ἀστροθέτην, σφραγῖδα δικαίαν
πόντου τ᾽ εἰναλίου καὶ γῆς, φύσεως τὸ βέβαιον
ἀκλινὲς ἀστασίαστον ἀεὶ τηροῦντα νόμοισιν,
οἷσιν ἄνωθε φέρων μέγαν οὐρανὸν αὐτὸς ὁδεύει,
καὶ φθόνον †οὐ δίκαιον† ῥοίζου τρόπον ἐκτὸς ἐλαύνει·
ὃς καὶ θνητοῖσιν βιοτῆς τέλος ἐσθλὸν ἐγείρει·
αὐτὸς γὰρ μοῦνος Ζώιων οἴακα κρατύνει
γνώμαις ὀρθοτάταισι συνών, ἀδιάστροφος αἰεί,
ὠγύγιος, πολύπειρος, ἀβλάπτως πᾶσι συνοικῶν

Honored by all and blissful, O bold and lofty
    Justice,
you are pure of thought and you reward propriety.
5   Your own conscience is unbreakable, for you break
    all
who do not submit to your yoke but...
in their greed upset the balance of your mighty
    scales.
Dauntless, charming, a lover of revel loved by all,
you rejoice in peace and you strive for a life
    that is stable.
10   You loathe unfairness but fairness delights you,
and in you knowledge of virtue reaches its noble
    goal.
Hear, O goddess, and rightly shatter wicked men,
that mortals who eat of this earth's fruits
and all the living creatures nursed in the bosom
15   of our divine mother, earth, and of the sea-
    dwelling Zeus
may follow a path both balanced and noble.

64. HYMN TO NOMOS

Upon the holy lord of men and gods I call,
heavenly Nomos who arranges the stars and sets a
    fair limit
between earth and the sea's waters and who by his
    laws
ever preserves nature's balance obedient and
    steady.
5   Journeying on the heavens he brings the laws from
    above
and drives malicious envy out with a roar.
Nomos summons a good end to mortal life
and he alone steers the course of everything
    that breathes,
ever the steadfast companion of righteous thought.

τοῖς νομίμοις, ἀνόμοις δὲ φέρων κακότητα βαρεῖαν.
ἀλλά, μάκαρ, πάντιμε, φερόλβιε, πᾶσι ποθεινέ,
εὐμενὲς ἦτορ ἔχων μνήμην σέο πέμπε, φέριστε.

65 Ἄρεος, θυμίαμα λίβανον.

Ἄρρηκτ', ὀμβριμόθυμε, μεγασθενές, ἄλκιμε δαῖμον,
ὁπλοχαρής, ἀδάμαστε, βροτοκτόνε, τειχεσιπλῆτα,
Ἄρες ἄναξ, ὁπλόδουπε, φόνοις πεπαλαγμένος αἰεί,
αἵματι ἀνδροφόνωι χαίρων, πολεμόκλονε, φρικτέ,
5   ὃς ποθέεις ξίφεσίν τε καὶ ἔγχεσι δῆριν ἄμουσον·
στῆσον ἔριν λυσσῶσαν, ἄνες πόνον ἀλγεσίθυμον,
εἰς δὲ πόθον νεῦσον Κύπριδος κώμους τε Λυαίου
ἀλλάξας ἀλκὴν ὅπλων εἰς ἔργα τὰ Δηοῦς,
εἰρήνην ποθέων κουροτρόφον, ὀλβιοδῶτιν.

66 Ἡφαίστου, θυμίαμα λιβανομάνναν.

Ἥφαιστ' ὀμβριμόθυμε, μεγασθενές, ἀκάματον πῦρ,
λαμπόμενε φλογέαις αὐγαῖς, φαεσίμβροτε δαῖμον,
φωσφόρε, καρτερόχειρ, αἰώνιε, τεχνοδίαιτε,

10 Primeval and wise, in peace he shares the same
        house with all
    who abide by the law, while he visits harsh
        vengeance upon the lawless.
    But, O blessed bringer of prosperity, beloved of
        all and honored,
    have kindness of heart and make me mindful of your
        lordship.

65. TO ARES,
incense - frankincense

    Unbreakable, strong-spirited, mighty and powerful
        demon,
    delighting in arms, indomitable, man-slaying, wall-
        battering;
    lord Ares, yours is the din of arms, and ever
        bespattered with blood
    you find joy in killing and in the fray of battle,
        O horrid one,
5   whose desire is for the rude clash of swords and
        spears.
    Stay the raging strife, relax pain's grip on my
        soul,
    and yield to the wish of Kypris and to the revels
        of Lyaios,
    exchanging the might of arms for the works of Deo,
    yearning for peace that nurtures youths and
        brings wealth.

66. TO HEPHAISTOS,
incense - powdered frankincense

    Powerful and strong-spirited Hephaistos,
        unwearying fire
    that shines in the gleam of flames, god bringing
        light
    to mortals, mighty-handed and eternal artisan.

5
ἐργαστήρ, κόσμοιο μέρος, στοιχεῖον ἀμεμφές,
παμφάγε, πανδαμάτωρ, πανυπέρτατε, παντοδίαιτε,
αἰθήρ, ἥλιος, ἄστρα, σελήνη, φῶς ἀμίαντον·
ταῦτα γὰρ Ἡφαίστοιο μέλη θνητοῖσι προφαίνει.
πάντα δὲ οἶκον ἔχεις, πᾶσαν πόλιν, ἔθνεα πάντα,
σώματά τε θνητῶν οἰκεῖς, πολύολβε, κραταιέ.

10
κλῦθι, μάκαρ, κλήιζω ⟨σε⟩ πρὸς εὐιέρους ἐπιλοιβάς,
αἰεὶ ὅπως χαίρουσιν ἐπ᾽ ἔργοις ἥμερος ἔλθοις.
παῦσον λυσσῶσαν μανίαν πυρὸς ἀκαμάτοιο
καῦσιν ἔχων φύσεως ἐν σώμασιν ἡμετέροισιν.

67 Ἀσκληπιοῦ, θυμίαμα μάνναν.

Ἰητὴρ πάντων, Ἀσκληπιέ, δέσποτα Παιάν,
θέλγων ἀνθρώπων πολυαλγέα πήματα νούσων,
ἠπιόδωρε, κραταιέ, μόλοις κατάγων ὑγίειαν
καὶ παύων νούσους, χαλεπὰς κῆρας θανάτοιο,

5
αὐξιθαλής, ἐπίκουρ᾽, ἀπαλεξίκακ᾽, ὀλβιόμοιρε,
Φοίβου Ἀπόλλωνος κρατερὸν θάλος ἀγλαότιμον,
ἐχθρὲ νόσων, Ὑγίειαν ἔχων σύλλεκτρον ἀμεμφῆ,
ἐλθέ, μάκαρ, σωτήρ, βιοτῆς τέλος ἐσθλὸν ὀπάζων.

68 Ὑγείας, θυμίαμα μάνναν.

Ἱμερόεσσ᾽, ἐρατή, πολυθάλμιε, παμβασίλεια,
κλῦθι, μάκαιρ᾽ Ὑγίεια, φερόλβιε, μῆτερ ἁπάντων·

Worker, cosmic part and blameless element,
5   highest of all, all-eating, all-taming and all-
         haunting,
ether, sun, stars, moon and pure light;
for it is a part of Hephaistos all these reveal
         to mortals.
All homes, all cities and all nations are yours,
and, O mighty giver of many blessings, you dwell
         in human bodies.
10   Hear me, lord, as I summon you to this holy
         libation,
that you may always come, gentle, to make work a
         joy.
End the savage rage of untiring fire
since, through you, nature itself burns in our
         bodies.

67. TO ASKLEPIOS,
incense - frankincense

Asklepios, lord Paian, healer of all,
you charm away the suffering of men in pain.
Come, mighty and soothing, bring health,
and put an end to sickness and the harsh fate of
         death.
5   Helper, blessed spirit of growth and blossoming,
         you ward evil off,
honored and mighty scion of Phoibos Apollon.
Enemy of disease, whose blameless consort is
         Hygieia,
come, O blessed one, as savior and bring life to
         a good end.

68. TO HYGEIA,
incense - frankincense

Queen of all, charming and lovely and blooming,
blessed Hygeia, mother of all, bringer of
         prosperity, hear me.

ἐκ σέο γὰρ νοῦσοι μὲν ἀποφθινύθουσι βροτοῖσι,
πᾶς δὲ δόμος θάλλει πολυγηθὴς εἵνεκα σεῖο,
καὶ τέχναι βρίθουσι· ποθεῖ δέ σε κόσμος, ἄνασσα,
μοῦνός δὲ στυγέει σ᾽ Ἀίδης ψυχοφθόρος αἰεί,
ἀιθαλής, εὐκταιοτάτη, θνητῶν ἀνάπαυμα·
σοῦ γὰρ ἄτερ πάντ᾽ ἐστὶν ἀνωφελῆ ἀνθρώποισιν·
οὔτε γὰρ ὀλβοδότης πλοῦτος γλυκερὸς θαλίηισιν,
οὔτε γέρων πολύμοχθος ἄτερ σέο γίγνεται ἀνήρ·
πάντων γὰρ κρατέεις μούνη καὶ πᾶσιν ἀνάσσεις.
ἀλλά, θεά, μόλε μυστιπόλοις ἐπιτάρροθος αἰεὶ
ῥυομένη νούσων χαλεπῶν κακόποτμον ἀνίην.

69 Ἐρινύων, θυμίαμα στύρακα καὶ μάνναν.

Κλῦτε, θεαὶ πάντιμοι, ἐρίβρομοι, εὐάστειραι,
Τισιφόνη τε καὶ Ἀλληκτὼ καὶ δῖα Μέγαιρα·
νυκτέριαι, μύχιαι, ὑπὸ κεύθεσιν οἰκί᾽ ἔχουσαι
ἄντρωι ἐν ἠερόεντι παρὰ Στυγὸς ἱερὸν ὕδωρ,
οὐχ ὁσίαις βουλαῖσι βροτῶν κεκοτημέναι αἰεί,
λυσσήρεις, ἀγέρωχοι, ἐπευάζουσαι ἀνάγκαις,
θηρόπεπλοι, τιμωροί, ἐρισθενέες, βαρυαλγεῖς,
Ἀίδεω χθόνιαι, φοβεραὶ κόραι, αἰολόμορφοι,
ἠέριαι, ἀφανεῖς, ὠκυδρόμοι ὥστε νόημα·
οὔτε γὰρ ἠελίου ταχιναὶ φλόγες οὔτε σελήνης
καὶ σοφίης ἀρετῆς τε καὶ ἐργασίμου θρασύτητος
† εὔχαρι οὔτε βίου λιπαρᾶς περικαλλέος ἥβης

Through you vanish the diseases that afflict men,
and through you every house blossoms to fullness
    of joy,
5   and the arts thrive. The world desires you, O
    queen,
and only soul-destroying Hades ever loathes you;
ever youthful, ever beloved, you are a haven for
    mortals.
Apart from you all is without avail for men:
wealth, sweet to those who feast, and giver of
    abundance, fails,
10   and man never reaches the many pains of old age,
for you are sole mistress and queen of all.
But, goddess, come, ever helpful to the initiates
and keep away the accursed distress of harsh
    disease.

69. TO THE ERINYES,
incense - storax -
powdered frankincense

Hear, Tisiphone, Allekto, and noble Megaira,
august goddesses whose Bacchic cries resound.
Nocturnal and clandestine, you have your house deep
    down
in a dank cave by the sacred water of the Styx.
5   Men's unholy designs incur your anger;
rabid and arrogant, you howl over Necessity's
    dictates
and, clad in animal skins, by your power you bring
    the deep pains of retribution.
Your realm is in Hades, O dreaded maidens with the
    thousand faces,
phantoms airy, invisible and swift as thought.
10   Neither the speedy flames of the sun or the moon,
nor the radiance of wisdom and virtue, nor even
    the joy
in bold enterprise as well as in the sleekness of
    fair youth

ὑμῶν χωρὶς ἐγείρει εὐφροσύνας βιότοιο·
ἀλλ' αἰεὶ θνητῶν πάντων ἐπ' ἀπείρονα φῦλα
15 ὄμμα Δίκης ἐφορᾶτε, δικασπόλοι αἰὲν ἐοῦσαι.
ἀλλά, θεαὶ Μοῖραι, ὀφιοπλόκαμοι, πολύμορφοι,
πραΰνοον μετάθεσθε βίου μαλακόφρονα δόξαν.

70 Εὐμενίδων, θυμίαμα ἀρώματα.

Κλῦτέ μου, Εὐμενίδες μεγαλώνυμοι, εὔφρονι βουλῆι,
ἁγναὶ θυγατέρες μεγάλοιο Διὸς χθονίοιο
Φερσεφόνης τ', ἐρατῆς κούρης καλλιπλοκάμοιο,
αἳ πάντων καθορᾶτε βίον θνητῶν ἀσεβούντων,
5 τῶν ἀδίκων τιμωροί, ἐφεστηκυῖαι ἀνάγκηι,
κυανόχρωτοι ἄνασσαι, ἀπαστράπτουσαι ἀπ' ὄσσων
δεινὴν ἀνταυγῆ φάεος σαρκοφθόρον αἴγλην·
ἀίδιοι, φοβερῶπες, ἀπόστροφοι, αὐτοκράτειραι,
λυσιμελεῖς οἴστρωι, βλοσυραί, νύχιαι, πολύποτμοι,
10 νυκτέριαι κοῦραι, ὀφιοπλόκαμοι, φοβερῶπες·
ὑμᾶς κικλήσκω γνώμαις ὁσίαισι πελάζειν.

71 Μηλινόης, θυμίαμα ἀρώματα.

Μηλινόην καλέω, νύμφην χθονίαν, κροκόπεπλον,
ἣν παρὰ Κωκυτοῦ προχοαῖς ἐλοχεύσατο σεμνὴ
Φερσεφόνη λέκτροις ἱεροῖς Ζηνὸς Κρονίοιο,
ἧι ψευσθεὶς Πλούτων' ἐμίγη δολίαις ἀπάταισι,
5 θυμῶι Φερσεφόνης δὲ δισώματον ἔσπασε χροιήν,

can arouse life's delights without your aid.
Upon the countless races of all men
15   you gaze as Dike's eye, ever occupied with
        justice.
O snake-haired, many-shaped goddesses of Fate,
change my thoughts of life into gentle and soft
        ones.

70. TO THE EUMENIDES,
incense - aromatic herbs

Hear me, renowned Eumenides, and be gracious;
pure daughters of the great chthonic Zeus
and of the lovely, fair-tressed maiden, Persephone.
You keep a watch over the lives of impious mortals
5   and, in charge of Necessity, you punish the unjust.
Black-skinned queens, your eyes flash forth awesome
and flesh-eating darts of light.
Everlasting, of visage repugnant and frightful,
        sovereign,
paralyzing the limbs with madness, hideous,
        nocturnal, fateful,
10   snake-haired and terrible maidens of the night,
it is you I summon to bring me holiness of mind.

71. TO MELINOE,
incense - aromatic herbs

I call upon Melinoe, saffron-cloaked nymph of the
        earth,
to whom august Persephone gave birth by the mouth
        of the Kokytos,
upon the sacred bed of Kronian Zeus.
He lied to Plouton and through treachery mated
        with Persephone,
5   whose skin when she was pregnant he mangled in
        anger.

ἢ θνητοὺς μαίνει φαντάσμασιν ἠερίοισιν,
ἀλλοκότοις ἰδέαις μορφῆς τύπον † ἐκπροφαίνουσα,
ἄλλοτε μὲν προφανής, ποτὲ δὲ σκοτόεσσα, νυχαυγής,
ἀνταίαις ἐφόδοισι κατὰ ζοφοειδέα νύκτα.
10 ἀλλά, θεά, λίτομαί σε, καταχθονίων βασίλεια,
ψυχῆς ἐκπέμπειν οἶστρον ἐπὶ τέρματα γαίης,
εὐμενὲς εὐίερον μύσταις φαίνουσα πρόσωπον.

72 Τύχης, θυμίαμα λίβανον.

Δεῦρο, Τύχη· καλέω σ', ἀγαθὴν κράντειραν, ἐπ' εὐχαῖς,
μειλιχίαν, ἐνοδῖτιν, ἐπ' εὐόλβοις κτεάτεσσιν,
Ἄρτεμιν ἡγεμόνην, μεγαλώνυμον, Εὐβουλῆος
αἵματος ἐκγεγαῶσαν, ἀπρό⟨σ⟩μαχον εὖχος ἔχουσαν,
5 τυμβιδίαν, πολύπλαγκτον, ἀοίδιμον ἀνθρώποισιν.
ἐν σοὶ γὰρ βίοτος θνητῶν παμποίκιλός ἐστιν·
οἷς μὲν γὰρ τεύχεις κτεάνων πλῆθος πολύολβον,
οἷς δὲ κακὴν πενίην θυμῶι χόλον ὁρμαίνουσα.
ἀλλά, θεά, λίτομαί σε μολεῖν βίωι εὐμενέουσαν,
10 ὄλβοισι πλήθουσαν ἐπ' εὐόλβοις κτεάτεσσιν.

She drives mortals to madness with her airy
    phantoms,
as she appears in weird shapes and forms,
now plain to the eye, now shadowy, now shining
    in the darkness -
and all this in hostile encounters in the gloom
    of night.
10   But goddess and queen of those below, I beseech
    you
to banish the soul's frenzy to the ends of the
    earth
and show a kindly and holy face to the initiates.

72. TO TYCHE,
incense - frankincense

With prayer in mind, I summon you here, Tyche,
    noble ruler,
gentle goddess of the roads, for wealth and
    possessions,
as Artemis who guides, renowned, sprung from the
    loins
of Eubouleus. Your wish is irresistible.
5   Funereal and delusive, you are the theme of men's
    songs.
In you lies the great variety of men's livelihood.
To some you grant a wealth of blessings and
    possessions,
while to others, against whom you harbor anger,
    you give evil poverty.
But, O goddess, I beseech you to come in kindness
    to my life
10   and with abundance grant me happiness and riches.

73 Δαίμονος, θυμίαμα λίβανον.

Δαίμονα κικλήσκω † μεγαλαν ἡγήτορα φρικτόν,
μειλίχιον Δία, παγγενέτην, βιοδώτορα θνητῶν,
Ζῆνα μέγαν, πολύπλαγκτον, ἀλάστορα, παμβασιλῆα,
πλουτοδότην, ὁπόταν γε βρυάζων οἶκον ἐσέλθηι,
ἔμπαλι δὲ τρύχοντα βίον θνητῶν πολυμόχθων·
ἐν σοὶ γὰρ λύπης τε χαρᾶς † κληῖδες ὀχοῦνται.
τοιγάρ τοι, μάκαρ, ἁγνέ, πολύστονα κήδε᾽ ἐλάσσας,
ὅσσα βιοφθορίην πέμπει κατὰ γαῖαν ἅπασαν,
ἔνδοξον βιοτῆς γλυκερὸν τέλος ἐσθλὸν ὀπάζοις.

74 Λευκοθέας, θυμίαμα ἀρώματα.

Λευκοθέαν καλέω Καδμηίδα, δαίμονα σεμνήν,
εὐδύνατον, θρέπτειραν ἐυστεφάνου Διονύσου.
κλῦθι, θεά, πόντοιο βαθυστέρνου μεδέουσα,
κύμασι τερπομένη, θνητῶν σώτειρα μεγίστη·
ἐν σοὶ γὰρ νηῶν πελαγοδρόμος ἄστατος ὁρμή,
μούνη δὲ θνητῶν οἰκτρὸν μόρον εἰν ἀλὶ λύεις,
οἷς ἂν ἐφορμαίνουσα φίλη σωτήριος ἔλθοις.
ἀλλά, θεὰ δέσποινα, μόλοις ἐπαρωγὸς ἐοῦσα
νηυσὶν ἐπ᾽ εὐσέλμοις σωτήριος εὔφρονι βουλῆι,
μύσταις ἐν πόντωι ναυσίδρομον οὖρον ἄγουσα.

73. TO THE DAIMON,
incense - frankincense

I call upon Daimon, the grand and dreaded chief-
    tain,
gentle Zeus, who gives birth and livelihood to
    mortals;
great Zeus, delusive and vengeful king of all,
who is giver of wealth when he enters the house,
    laden with goods,
5   and who in turn ruins the livelihood of toiling
    mortals.
You possess the keys to joy and sorrow as well.
So, O pure and blessed one, drive painful cares
    away,
cares that are life-destroying throughout the
    earth,
and bring a glorious, sweet and noble end to life.

74. TO LEUKOTHEA,
incense - aromatic herbs

I call upon Leukothea, daughter of Kadmos,
    reverend goddess,
mighty nurturer of fair-wreathed Dionysos.
Hearken, O goddess, mistress of the deep-bosomed
    sea,
you who delight in waves and are to mortals the
    greatest savior.
5   On you depends the unsteady impetus of seafaring
    ships,
and you alone save men from wretched death at sea,
men to whom you swiftly come as welcome savior.
But, O divine lady, come to the aid
of well-benched ships and kindly save them,
10   bringing upon the sea a fair tail wind to the
    initiates.

75 Παλαίμονος, θυμίαμα μάνναν.

Σύντροφε βακχεχόροιο Διωνύσου πολυγηθοῦς,
ὃς ναίεις πόντοιο βυθοὺς ἁλικύμονας, ἁγνούς,
κικλήσκω σε, Παλαῖμον, ἐπ᾽ εὐιέροις τελεταῖσιν
ἐλθεῖν εὐμενέοντα, νέωι γήθοντα προσώπωι,
5 καὶ σώζειν μύστας κατά τε χθόνα καὶ κατὰ πόντον·
ποντοπλάνοις γὰρ ἀεὶ ναυσὶν χειμῶνος ἐναργὴς
φαινομένου σωτὴρ μοῦνος θνητοῖς ἀναφαίνηι,
ῥυόμενος μῆνιν χαλεπὴν κατὰ πόντιον οἶδμα.

76 Μουσῶν, θυμίαμα λίβανον.

Μνημοσύνης καὶ Ζηνὸς ἐριγδούποιο θύγατρες,
Μοῦσαι Πιερίδες, μεγαλώνυμοι, ἀγλαόφημοι,
θνητοῖς, οἷς κε παρῆτε, ποθεινόταται, πολύμορφοι,
πάσης παιδείης ἀρετὴν γεννῶσαι ἄμεμπτον,
5 θρέπτειραι ψυχῆς, διανοίας ὀρθοδότειραι,
καὶ νόου εὐδυνάτοιο καθηγήτειραι ἄνασσαι,
αἳ τελετὰς θνητοῖς ἀνεδείξατε μυστιπ⟨ο⟩λεύτους,
Κλειώ τ᾽ Εὐτέρπη τε Θάλειά τε Μελπομένη τε
Τερψιχόρη τ᾽ Ἐρατώ τε Πολύμνιά τ᾽ Οὐρανίη τε
10 Καλλιόπηι σὺν μητρὶ καὶ εὐδυνάτηι θεᾶι Ἁγνῆι.
ἀλλὰ μόλοιτε, θεαί, μύσταις, πολυποίκιλοι, ἁγναί,
εὔκλειαν Ζῆλόν τ᾽ ἐρατὸν πολύυμνον ἄγουσαι.

77 Μνημοσύνης, θυμίαμα λίβανον

Μνημοσύνην καλέω, Ζηνὸς σύλλεκτρον, ἄνασσαν,
ἣ Μούσας τέκνωσ᾽ ἱεράς, ὁσίας, λιγυφώνους,

75. TO PALAIMON,
incense - powdered frankincense

Comrade of joyous Dionysos in the dance revel,
who dwell in the sea's pure, turbulent depths,
I call upon you, O Palaimon, to come to these
    sacred rites,
with kindness in your heart and joy on your
    youthful face,
5   and to save your initiates on land and at sea.
When in winter storms come upon ships that ever
    rove the seas
you alone appear incarnate to save the men
and stay the harsh anger over the briny swell.

76. TO THE MUSES,
incense - frankincense

Daughters of Mnemosyne and thundering Zeus,
Pierian Muses, renowned, illustrious,
many-shaped and beloved of the mortals you visit.
You give birth to unblemished virtue in every
    discipline,
5   you nourish the soul and set thought aright,
as you become leaders and mistresses of the mind's
    power.
Sacred and mystic rites you taught to mortals,
Kleio, Euterpe, Thaleia, Melpomene,
Terpsichore, Erato, Polymnia, Ourania
10   mother Kalliope, and mighty goddess Agne.
Do come to the initiates, O goddesses, in your
    manifold holiness,
and bring glory and emulation that is lovely and
    sung by many.

77. TO MNEMOSYNE,
incense - frankincense

I call upon queen Mnemosyne, Zeus' consort,
who gave birth to the holy, sacred and clear-
    voiced Muses.

ἐκτὸς ἐοῦσα κακῆς λήθης βλαψίφρονος αἰεί,
πάντα νόον συνέχουσα βροτῶν ψυχαῖσι σύνοικον,
5 εὐδύνατον κρατερὸν θνητῶν αὔξουσα λογισμόν,
ἡδυτάτη, φιλάγρυπνος ὑπομνήσκουσά τε πάντα,
ὧν ἂν ἕκαστος ἀεὶ στέρνοις γνώμην κατ⟨ά⟩θηται,
οὔτι παρεκβαίνουσ᾿, ἐπεγείρουσα φρένα πᾶσιν.
ἀλλά, μάκαιρα θεά, μύσταις μνήμην ἐπέγειρε
10 εὐιέρου τελετῆς, λήθην δ᾿ ἀπὸ τῶν⟨δ᾿⟩ ἀπόπεμπε.

78 Ἠοῦς, θυμίαμα μάνναν.

Κλῦθι, θεά, θνητοῖς φαεσίμβροτον ἦμαρ ἄγουσα,
Ἠὼς λαμπροφαής, ἐρυθαινομένη κατὰ κόσμον,
ἀγγέλτειρα θεοῦ μεγάλου Τιτᾶνος ἀγαυοῦ,
ἣ νυκτὸς ζοφόεντα κελαινόχρωτα πορείην
5 ἀντολίαις ταῖς σαῖς πέμπεις ὑπὸ νέρτερα γαίης·
ἔργων ἡγήτειρα, βίου πρόπολε θνητοῖσιν·
ἧι χαίρει θνητῶν μερόπων γένος· οὐδέ τίς ἐστιν,
ὃς φεύγει τὴν σὴν ὄψιν καθυπέρτερον οὖσαν,
ἡνίκα τὸν γλυκὺν ὕπνον ἀπὸ βλεφάρων ἀποσείσῃς,
10 πᾶς δὲ βροτὸς γήθει, πᾶν ἑρπετὸν ἄλλα τε φῦλα
τετραπόδων πτηνῶν τε καὶ εἰναλίων πολυεθνῶν·
πάντα γὰρ ἐργάσιμον βίοτον θνητοῖσι πορίζεις.
ἀλλά, μάκαιρ᾿, ἁγνή, μύσταις ἱερὸν φάος αὔξοις.

79 Θέμιδος, θυμίαμα λίβανον.

Οὐρανόπαιδ᾿ ἁγνὴν καλέω Θέμιν εὐπατέρειαν,
Γαίης τὸ βλάστημα, νέην καλυκώπιδα κούρην,
ἣ πρώτη κατέδειξε βροτοῖς μαντήιον ἁγνὸν

Evil oblivion that harms the mind is alien to her
who gives coherence to the mind and soul of
   mortals.
5   She increases men's ability and power to think,
and, sweet and vigilant, she reminds us of all
the thoughts that we always store in our breasts,
never straying, and ever rousing the mind to
   action.
But, O blessed goddess, for the initiates stir the
   memory
10   of the sacred rite, and ward off oblivion from
   them.

78. TO DAWN,
incense - powdered frankincense

Hear, O goddess who brings the light of day to
   mortals,
resplendent Dawn, whose blush is seen throughout
   the world,
messenger of the great and illustrious Titan.
Murky, dark, and journeying night
5   you send below the earth when you rise.
You lead to work and minister to the lives of
   mortals.
In you the race of mortal men delights, and no one
escapes your sight, as you look down from on high,
when from your eyelids you shake off sweet sleep.
10   There is joy then for every mortal, every reptile,
for animals and birds, and for the broods the sea
   contains.
All livelihood one gets from work is your gift.
So, goddess blessed and pure, give more sacred
   light to the initiates.

79. TO THEMIS,
incense - frankincense

I call upon pure Themis, daughter of noble Ouranos
and Gaia, Themis the young and lovely-faced maiden,
the first to show mortals the holy oracle

Δελφικῶι ἐν κευθμῶνι θεμιστεύουσα θεοῖσ⟨ι⟩
Πυθίωι ἐν δαπέδωι, ὅθι Πύθων ἐμβασίλευεν·
ἢ καὶ Φοῖβον ἄνακτα θεμιστοσύνας ἐδίδαξε·
πάντιμ᾽, ἀγλαόμορφε, σεβάσμιε, νυκτιπόλευτε·
πρώτη γὰρ τελετὰς ἁγίας θνητοῖς ἀνέφηνας,
βακχιακὰς ἀνὰ νύκτας ἐπευάζουσα ἄνακτα·
ἐκ σέο γὰρ τιμαὶ μακάρων μυστήριά θ᾽ ἁγνά.
ἀλλά, μάκαιρ᾽, ἔλθοις κεχαρημένη εὔφρονι βουλῆι
εὐιέρους ἐπὶ μυστιπόλους τελετὰς σέο, κούρη.

80 Βορέου, θυμίαμα λίβανον.

Χειμερίοις αὔραισι δονῶν βαθὺν ἠέρα κόσμου,
κρυμοπαγὴς Βορέα, χιονώδεος ἔλθ᾽ ἀπὸ Θράικης
λῦέ τε παννέφελον στάσιν ἠέρος ὑγροκελεύθου
ῥιπίζων ἱκμάσιν νοτεραῖς ὀμβρηγενὲς ὕδωρ,
αἴθρια πάντα τιθείς, θαλερόμματον αἰθέρα τεύχων
† ἀκτίνες ὣς λάμπουσιν † ἐπὶ χθονὸς ἠελίοιο.

81 Ζεφύρου, θυμίαμα λίβανον.

Αὖραι παντογενεῖς Ζεφυρίτιδες, ἠεροφοῖται,
ἡδύπνοοι, ψιθυραί, † θανάτου ἀνάπαυσιν ἔχουσαι,
εἰαριναί, λειμωνιάδες, πεποθημέναι ὅρμοις,
σύρουσαι ναυσὶ τρυφερὸν † ὅρμον, ἠέρα κοῦφον·
ἔλθοιτ᾽ εὐμενέουσαι, ἐπιπνείουσαι ἀμεμφεῖς,
ἠέριαι, ἀφανεῖς, κουφόπτεροι, ἀερόμορφοι.

as prophet of the gods in her Delphic sanctuary,
5 on Pythian ground, where Python was king.
You taught lord Phoibos the art of giving laws.
Amid honor and reverence, your beauty shines on
    nightly throngs,
for you were first to show mortals holy worship,
howling to Bacchos in nights full of revelry.
10 From you come the honors of the gods and the holy
    mysteries.
But, O blessed maiden, come in a kindly and joyous
    spirit
to your truly holy and mystic rites.

80. TO BOREAS,
incense - frankincense

Freezing Boreas, whose wintry breezes make the
    world's
lofty air quiver, come away from snowy Thrace!
Dissolve the rebellious alliance of clouds and
    moist air,
and turn the water to rushing drops of rain.
5 Bring fair weather everywhere, and give ether its
    bright eye,
the sun, whose rays shine upon the earth.

81. TO ZEPHYROS,
incense - frankincense

Western breezes, ethereal begetters of all,
as you blow gently your whisper brings deathlike
    rest.
Vernal and meadow-haunting, you are loved by havens
because to ships you bring ... soft and light air.
5 Come in a spirit of kindness and blow perfectly,
O airy, invisible and light-winged ones.

82 Νότου, θυμίαμα λίβανον.

Λαιψηρὸν πήδημα δι' ἠέρος ὑγροπόρευτον,
ὠκείαις πτερύγεσσι δονούμενον ἔνθα καὶ ἔνθα,
ἔλθοις σὺν νεφέλαις νοτίαις, ὄμβροιο γενάρχα·
τοῦτο γὰρ ἐκ Διός ἐστι σέθεν γέρας ἠερόφοιτον,
ὀμβροτόκους νεφέλας ἐξ ἠέρος εἰς χθόνα πέμπειν.
τοιγάρ τοι λιτόμεσθα, μάκαρ, ἱεροῖσι χαρέντα
πέμπειν καρποτρόφους ὄμβρους ἐπὶ μητέρα γαῖαν.

83 Ὠκεανοῦ, θυμίαμα ἀρώματα.

Ὠκεανὸν καλέω, πατέρ' ἄφθιτον, αἰὲν ἐόντα,
ἀθανάτων τε θεῶν γένεσιν θνητῶν τ' ἀνθρώπων,
ὃς περικυμαίνει γαίης περιτέρμονα κύκλον·
ἐξ οὗπερ πάντες ποταμοὶ καὶ πᾶσα θάλασσα
καὶ χθόνιοι γαίης πηγόρρυτοι ἰκμάδες ἁγναί.
κλῦθι, μάκαρ, πολύολβε, θεῶν ἅγνισμα μέγιστον,
τέρμα φίλον γαίης, ἀρχὴ πόλου, ὑγροκέλευθε,
ἔλθοις εὐμενέων μύσταις κεχαρισμένος αἰεί.

84 Ἑστίας, θυμίαμα ἀρώματα.

Ἑστία εὐδυνάτοιο Κρόνου θύγατερ βασίλεια,
ἡ μέσον οἶκον ἔχεις πυρὸς ἀενάοιο, μεγίστου,
τούσδε σὺ ἐν τελεταῖς ὁσίους μύστας ἀναδείξαις,
θεῖσ' αἰειθαλέας, πολυόλβους, εὔφρονας, ἁγνούς·
οἶκε θεῶν μακάρων, θνητῶν στήριγμα κραταιόν,
ἀιδίη, πολύμορφε, ποθεινοτάτη, χλοόμορφε·

82. TO NOTOS,
incense - frankincense

Quickly leaping through the moist air,
and with both of your swift wings vibrating,
come, father of rain, with the southern clouds.
Zeus did give you this lofty prerogative,
5   to send the rain-giving clouds from sky to earth.
Hence, we pray to you, O blessed one, to take
    delight
in our sacrifice and send fruit-nourishing rains
    to mother earth.

83. TO OKEANOS,
incense - aromatic herbs

I summon Okeanos, ageless and eternal father,
begetter of immortal gods and mortal men,
Okeanos who with his waves encircles the earth.
From him come every sea and every river
5   and so do the pure and flowing waters of earth's
    springs.
Hear me, O blessed god and highest divine
    purifier,
- the earth's own end, the pole's beginning, where
    the ships glide on -
and come, kind and ever gracious, to the initiates.

84. TO HESTIA,
incense - aromatic herbs

Queen Hestia, daughter of mighty Kronos,
mistress of ever burning and peerless fire, you
    dwell in the house center.
May you hallow the initiates of these rites and
    grant them
unwithering youth, riches, prudence, and purity.
5   You are the home of the blessed gods, and men's
    mighty buttress,
eternal, many-shaped, beloved, and grass-yellow.

μειδιόωσα, μάκαιρα, τάδ᾽ ἱερὰ δέξο προθύμως,
ὄλβον ἐπιπνείουσα καὶ ἠπιόχειρον ὑγείαν.

85 Ὕπνου, θυμίαμα μετὰ μήκωνος.

Ὕπνε, ἄναξ μακάρων πάντων θνητῶν τ᾽ ἀνθρώπων
καὶ πάντων ζώιων, ὁπόσα τρέφει εὐρεῖα χθών·
πάντων γὰρ κρατέεις μοῦνος καὶ πᾶσι προσέρχηι
σώματα δεσμεύων ἐν ἀχαλκεύτοισι πέδηισι,
5 λυσιμέριμνε, κόπων ἡδεῖαν ἔχων ἀνάπαυσιν
καὶ πάσης λύπης ἱερὸν παραμύθιον ἔρδων·
καὶ θανάτου μελέτην ἐπάγεις ψυχὰς διασώζων·
αὐτοκασίγνητος γὰρ ἔφυς Λήθης Θανάτου τε.
ἀλλά, μάκαρ, λίτομαί σε κεκραμένον ἡδὺν ἱκάνειν
10 σώζοντ᾽ εὐμενέως μύστας θείοισιν ἐπ᾽ ἔργοις.

86 Ὀνείρου, θυμίαμα ἀρώματα.

Κικλήσκω σε, μάκαρ, τανυσίπτερε, οὖλε Ὄνειρε,
ἄγγελε μελλόντων, θνητοῖς χρησμωιδὲ μέγιστε·
ἡσυχίαι γὰρ ὕπνου γλυκεροῦ σιγηλὸς ἐπελθών,
προ⟨σ⟩φωνῶν ψυχαῖς θνητῶν νόον αὐτὸς ἐγείρεις,
5 καὶ γνώμας μακάρων αὐτὸς καθ᾽ ὕπνους ὑποπέμπεις,

Smile, O blessed one, and kindly accept these
offerings,
wafting upon us prosperity and gentle-handed
health.

85.   TO SLEEP,
incense with opium poppy

Sleep, you are lord of all the blessed gods and
mortal men,
and of every living creature the broad earth
nurtures,
for you alone are master of all and you visit all,
binding their bodies with fetters unforged.
5   You free us of cares, and offering sweet respite
from toil
you grant holy solace to our every sorrow.
You save souls by easing them into the thought of
death
since to Death and Oblivion you are a true
brother.
But, O blessed one, I beseech you to come, sweet-
tempered,
10   and kindly save the initiates, that they may serve
the gods.

86.   TO DREAM,
incense - aromatic herbs

I call upon you, blessed, long-winged and baneful
Dream,
messenger of things to come, greatest prophet to
mortals.
In the quiet of sweet sleep you come silently
and, speaking to the soul, you rouse men's minds
5   and in their sleep you whisper to them the will of
the blessed ones.

σιγῶν σιγώσαις ψυχαῖς μέλλοντα προφαίνων,
οἶσιν ἐπ' εὐσεβίηισι θεῶν νόος ἐσθλὸς ὁδεύει,
ὡς ἂν ἀεὶ τὸ καλὸν μᾶλλον, γνώμηισι προληφθέν,
τερπωλαῖς ὑπάγηι βίον ἀνθρώπων προχαρέντων,

10 τῶν δὲ κακῶν ἀνάπαυλαν, ὅπως θεὸς αὐτὸς †ἐνίσπηι
εὐχωλαῖς θυσίαις τε †πόλον θύσαντες† ἀνάκτων.
εὐσεβέσιν γὰρ ἀεὶ τὸ τέλος γλυκερώτερόν ἐστι,
τοῖς δὲ κακοῖς οὐδὲν φαίνει μέλλουσαν ἀνάγκην
ὄψις ὀνειρήεσσα, κακῶν ἐξάγγελος ἔργων,

15 ὄφρα †ἂν εὕρωνται λύσιν ἄλγεος ἐρχομένοιο.
ἀλλά, μάκαρ, λίτομαί σε θεῶν μηνύματα φράζειν,
ὡς ἂν ἀεὶ γνώμαις ὀρθαῖς κατὰ πάντα πελάζηις
μηδὲν ἐπ' ἀλλοκότοισι κακῶν σημεῖα προφαίνων.

87 Θανάτου, θυμίαμα μάνναν.

Κλῦθί μευ, ὃς πάντων θνητῶν οἴηκα κρατύνεις
πᾶσι διδοὺς χρόνον ἁγνόν, ὅσων πόρρωθεν ὑπάρχεις·
σὸς γὰρ ὕπνος ψυχὴν θραύει καὶ σώματος ὁλκόν,
ἡνίκ' ἂν ἐκλύηις φύσεως κεκρατημένα δεσμὰ

5 τὸν μακρὸν ζώιοισι φέρων αἰώνιον ὕπνον,
κοινὸς μὲν πάντων, ἄδικος δ' ἐνίοισιν ὑπάρχων,
ἐν ταχυτῆτι βίου παύων νεοήλικας ἀκμάς·
ἐν σοὶ γὰρ μούνωι πάντων τὸ κριθὲν τελεοῦται·
οὔτε γὰρ εὐχαῖσιν πείθηι μόνος οὔτε λιταῖσιν.

10 ἀλλά, μάκαρ, μακροῖσι χρόνοις ζωῆς σε πελάζειν
αἰτοῦμαι, θυσίαις⟨ι⟩ καὶ εὐχωλαῖς λιτανεύων,
ὡς ἂν ἔοι γέρας ἐσθλὸν ἐν ἀνθρώποισι τὸ γῆρας.

Silent you come to show the future to silent souls
that walk on the noble path of piety to the gods,
so that always good wins the race to people's
    minds
and leads their lives to pleasures enjoyed before
    evil arrives
10   and to a respite from suffering. . . . .
    . . . .
The end to which the pious come is always sweeter
but to the impious never does a dreamy phantom,
a prophet of evil deeds, reveal future necessity,
15   so that they may find deliverance from pain to
    come.
But blessed one, I beg you to show me the behests
    of the gods
and in all things bring me close to the straight
    path.
Do not show me evil signs which conduce to mon-
    strous deeds.

87. TO DEATH,
incense - powdered frankincense

Hear me you who steer the course of all mortals
and give holy time to all ahead of whom you lie.
Your sleep tears the soul free from the body's hold
when you undo nature's tenacious bonds,
5   bringing long and eternal slumber to the living.
Common to all, you are unjust to some
when you bring a swift end to youthful life at its
    peak.
In you alone is the verdict common to all executed,
for to prayers and entreaties you alone are deaf.
10   But, O blessed one, with sacrifices and pious vows
I beg you to grant long life,
that old age might be a noble prize among men.

NOTES

ORPHEUS TO MOUSAIOS

1. Orpheus, who addresses Mousaios here, was a legendary Thracian singer of supernatural charm, and the
   founder of Orphism. Readers will recall how he descended to the Underworld to bring back his wife,
   Eurydike, and how, according to another legend, he
   met with tragic death in the hands of Thracian men-
   ads who tore his body to pieces. The fragments of
   poetry attributed to Orpheus have been published by
   Otto Kern in his *Orphicorum Fragmenta* (1922).
   Mousaios is an equally legendary singer of great
   fame and, presumably, a contemporary of Orpheus (see
   Aristophanes, *Frogs* 1032-3, and Plato, *Republic*
   364e).

3. Gaia is the Earth. For Gaia's position in Greek
   theogony and cosmogony see Hesiod, *Theogony* 116ff.

11. The foam-born goddess is Aphrodite.

12. Plouton is meant.

13. Hebe is daughter of Zeus and Hera, sister of Ares
    and Eileithyia (about her see notes on 2).

19. Leto, daughter of Koios and Phoibe, is a Titaness
    (Hesiod, *Theogony* 404ff.). Dione is Zeus' consort
    and mother of Aphrodite. From her name one might
    conjecture that she is a sky goddess, eventually
    ousted by Hera.

20. On the Kouretes and Korybantes see notes on 31, 38,
    39. The Kabeiroi were chthonic gods, possibly of
    Phrygian origin. They were connected with Demeter,
    Dionysos and Hermes, and their principal center of
    worship was at Samothrace (see also Herodotos, 2.51).

22. The Idaian gods must be the so-called Idaian Daktyls
    about whose size and identity there was great doubt
    in antiquity. Some thought they came from the Cre-
    tan Ida, others from the Phrygian one. According to
    the oldest tradition, preserved in the *Phoronis,*

they were mountain giants and inventors of smith-
craft.

23. Themis, daughter of Gaia (perhaps also an earlier
double for Gaia), was Zeus' second consort
(Hesiod, *Theogony* 135, 901).

25-27. Dike is Justice personified. In Hesiod, *Theogony*
902 she is one of the Horai. Thesmodoteira = she
that gives laws. Rhea and Kronos are the parents
of most Olympian gods, including Zeus (Hesiod,
Theogony 453ff.). Tethys is the bride of Okeanos,
and by him the mother of the Okeanidai (Hesiod,
Theogony 337ff.).

28. Atlas, a Titan, is son of Iapetos and Klymene.
He supports the sky on his shoulders (Hesiod,
Theogony 509, 517). Aion, personification of a
period of time, is a late-comer to cult, and his
connections may be both Orphic and Mithraic.

29. Chronos, 'Time', is frequently equated with Kronos in Orphism. Styx, an Arcadian river, was one
of the nine rivers of the Underworld. Gods frequently swore by it (so Hera in *Iliad* 15.37), and
their oaths were irrevocable.

30. For Pronoia see Introduction.

35. Ino is daughter of Kadmos and wife of Athamas.
According to one tradition she had nursed Dionysos
and this angered Hera, who then drove Athamas and
her mad. She ran from her insane husband and,
carrying Melikertes, her son, she leaped into the
sea, where she and her son were transformed into
the deities Leukothea and Palaimon respectively.

36. Adresteia is a Traco-Phrygian mountain goddess
and mother of the Idaian Daktyls. In Orphic belief she is an Underworld figure, not infrequently identified with Ananke.

40. Attis, originally a Phrygian vegetation god, is
the consort of Kybele. Men is an obscure Phrygian goddess.

1 - TO HEKATE

Hekate is a goddess especially connected with magic and superstition. She was frequently confused with Artemis and even with Selene. She is the daughter of Perses and Asterie and in Hesiod she is depicted as a powerful and benign goddess and not as hideous demon (*Theogony* 411ff.). The epithet σκυλακῖτις (5) literally means 'of whelps' or 'of dogs', and may not be unrelated to the practice of offering dog flesh as one of the ingredients of her "suppers". The epithet κουροτρόφος, 'nurturer of youths', is at least as old as Hesiod (*Theogony* 450), and she shares it with Artemis. The 'oxherd' (βουκόλος) of line 10 must have been a high official of an Orphic association. This much we learn from inscriptions of the Roman period, unearthed in Asia Minor.

2 - TO PROTHYRAIA

Prothyraia literally means 'at the door' or 'at the door-way'. There is no goddess proper by this name. The word is a cult title shared by Eileithyia, Artemis, and even Hekate (*Procli H.* 6.2 and 14). In this hymn Artemis and Eileithyia are treated as two faces of the same goddess of childbirth, a divinity which seems to go back to Minoan-Mycenaean times. It would be interesting to explore whether the name Eileithyia was originally a cult title of Artemis and whether Artemis herself, otherwise the virgin goddess par excellence, was originally associated with childbirth and fertility (cf. λυσίζωνος, 'looser of girdles' in line 7) in her august role as πότνια θηρῶν, 'mistress of wild beasts.'

3 - TO NIGHT

Night (Nyx) is personified in Hesiod. She is the daughter of Chaos and the sister of Erebos. It is interesting that Αἰθήρ (Ether) and Ἡμέρη (Day) are children of night (*Theogony* 123-4). It is equally interesting that

in the Bible God creates light out of darkness. In *Iliad*
14.259 she is called δμήτειρα θεῶν, 'tamer of the gods',
a phrase which points to primeval night. In the *Rhapsodic
Theogony* she is the daughter of Phanes, the creator, and
assumes a power of supremacy which continues unchallenged
through the reigns of Ouranos, Kronos, and Zeus.

4 - TO OURANOS

In Hesiod's *Theogony* Ouranos is son and husband of
Gaia (126ff.), and Kronos is their son who, in fact, con-
spired with Gaia to castrate his father. In the *Orphic
Theogony* Phanes and Night beget Gaia and Ouranos; these
two, in turn, beget Kronos, Rhea, etc. Eventually, Night
gave her supreme power to Ouranos. Φύσις, 'nature', and
ἀνάγκη, 'necessity' ('drive') in line 6 would be pregnant
with meaning for the Orphic (see introduction).

5 - TO ETHER

Ether is the child of Chronos (Time) by Ananke.
Chaos and Erebos are his siblings. It is in Ether that
Chronos places the primeval egg out of which Phanes is
born. In Hesiod Ether is the son of Erebos and Night
(*Theogony* 124-5). He is, as usual, identified with the
higher and hence purer stratum of air.

6 - TO PROTOGONOS

Protogonos and Erikepaios and here Antauges are at-
tributes of Phanes. Protogonos means the 'first-born'
and Antauges 'The One Reflecting Light'. Erikepaios is
obscure. As has been mentioned above Phanes is born of
the egg that Chronos places in Ether. According to Orphic
belief it is Phanes who is the creator of All, since even
Gaia (Earth) and Ouranos (Sky) are his children from
Night, his own daughter. Phanes is portrayed with golden
wings. In a celebrated passage from the *Birds* of Aristophanes golden-winged Eros is born from an egg which Night

places in the bosom of Erebos (693 ff).

7 - TO THE STARS

In Hesiod it is the Dawn ('Ηώς) which gives birth to
the Stars (378 ff.). Here they are called "children of
dark Night," and in consonance with astrological belief,
they govern men's fate. The "seven luminous orbits" of
line 8 are, of course, the seven planetary zones. Aris-
totle in *de Mund.* 2 gives the following order of the
planets: Saturn, Jupiter, Mars, Mercury, Venus, Sun,
Moon. The "learned contests" of line 12 might possibly
have been contests in which initiates would display their
knowledge of Orphism.

8 - TO THE SUN

Compare this hymn with *Homeric Hymn* 31. There the
Sun (Helios) is the son of Hyperion and Euryphaessa. In
Hesiod it is Theia who gives birth to Helios, Selene
(Moon) and Eos (Dawn): *Theogony* 371-4. The concept of
the Sun as charioteer is not found in the *Iliad* or *Odyssey*, but it is common in the *Homeric Hymns* (2.63 and 68;
4.69; 28.14). The identification with Apollon is clearer
here than in the *Homeric Hymn*. The expressions "cosmic
eye" (14) and "eye of justice" (18) go back to the more
basic idea that the sun sees and hears all things (so in
Iliad 3.277).

9 - TO THE MOON

This hymn should be compared with *Homeric Hymn* 32.
Throughout it there are indications of the identification
of Selene (Moon) with Hekate and, perhaps, even with
Artemis. She is "all-seeing, vigilant" (7), and those
familiar with the *Homeric Hymn to Demeter* will remember
how Persephone's cry did not escape Helios and Hekate,
who is definitely identified with the Moon (24 ff.).
Evident also in this hymn are her connections with sexu-

ality and fertility. The expression "in three ways shine
your redeeming light" (11/12) must refer to the waxing,
full, and waning moon. Hesiod divides the lunar month
into three thirds, φθίνων, 'waning', μέσσος, 'middle',
and ἱστάμενος, 'standing' (cf. *Works and Days* 795, 798).

10 - TO PHYSIS

Physis (Nature) was conceived by the Greeks, since
early times, as the vaguely personified sum total of the
creative powers or creative genius of the cosmos at work.
All major philosophical schools had their theories on its
modus operandi, but there is next to nothing in this hymn
to help us ascribe it to a particular religious or philo-
sophic tradition.

11 - TO PAN

In the more beautiful *Homeric Hymn* 19, Pan is a wan-
ton and sportive god of the Arcadian woodlands. Here he
has not altogether lost his character, but he is elevated
to the position of a "veritable Zeus with horns" (12), of
a musician who "weaves his song into cosmic harmony," of
a spirit of vegetation that nourishes mankind (20) and,
with allusions to a folk etymology of his name (πᾶν =
'all', in Greek), of lord of sky, land, and sea.

12 - TO HERAKLES

Herakles is not, strictly speaking, a Titan. For the
circumstances of his birth see Hesiod *Shield* 1-54. The
phrase you "change your form" (3) must refer to the fact
that he was frequently identified with foreign gods (cf.
Herodotos 2.43). "Father of time" in line 3 is difficult
to understand, and the cult epithet Paion (usually Paian
or Paieon), properly belongs to Apollon. Herakles was
worshiped as a hero, and only occasionally as god. The
last four lines are consonant with the hero's role in
private worship. Quite characteristically, the hymn is
syncretistic, and it elevates Herakles even above the

eminent status he enjoyed among Stoics and Cynics.

13 - TO KRONOS

Orphism quite early identified Kronos with Chronos
(Time). As Chronos, he is indeed father of gods and men,
since he sired the primeval elements, Chaos, Erebos and
Ether. Within Ether he placed the primeval egg out of
which Phanes, the Creator, came. It is according to the
Hesiodic *Theogony* that Kronos is a son of Ouranos (Sky)
and Gaia (Earth). Line 6, however, in addition to allud-
ing to that, is also a variant of the well-known Orphic
line from the gold plate of Petelia, South Italy (4th -
3rd c. B.C.). When the dead man reaches the spring flowing from the Lake of Memory, he must tell its guardians
"I am a child of Earth and of Starry Sky."

14 - TO RHEA

Strictly speaking, Rhea is granddaughter of Phanes
(Protogonos according to Orphic belief) and Night, and
daughter of Ouranos and Gaia. She is indeed wife of Kronos and, therefore, mother of Zeus (cf. Hesiod, *Theogony*
133-5; 453-8; 625; 634). Rhea is identified with Demeter,
Kybele, and quite fittingly with the Mother of the Gods
(cf. Hymn 27). In fact, this hymn bears a strong resem-
blance to *Homeric Hymn* 14. Lines 10-11 elevate her to the
status of the primeval womb of all creation.

15 - TO ZEUS

In this hymn Zeus has some of his traditional attri-
butes, but at the same time he is the primeval creator of
all, or in the words of line 6 "father of all, beginning
and end of all."

16 - TO HERA

Much as in the preceding hymn in which Zeus is the
primeval father of all, Hera is the primeval mother of
all. However, unlike Rhea, most scholars consider her a
sky goddess.

17 - TO POSEIDON

For the tripartite division of the world see *Iliad*
15.186-91. Usually it is the Dioskouroi who are saviors
of ships (cf. *Homeric Hymn* 33). For Poseidon's equestrian character see *Iliad* 23.307; Sophocles *Oedipus Col.*
712-15; Aristophanes *Knights* 551-58.

18 - TO PLOUTON

The expression "chthonic Zeus" (3) does not imply
that Zeus and Plouton are the same person but, rather,
that Plouton is lord of his own element, the depths of
the earth, and by extension of the whole earth. The re-
semblance between the name Plouton and the word *Ploutos*
(wealth) may have contributed to the idea expressed in
line 5, but Plouton, as master of the dark forces beneath
the surface of the earth and as consort of Persephone, has
indeed serious claims to the powers of fertility. For
line 6 see *Iliad* 15.191. According to *Iliad* 15.191 Hades
(here Plouton) received the overlordship of "misty darkness". Earth and Olympos were to be shared by Zeus,
Poseidon and Hades (193). Perhaps line 6 of this hymn is
meant to emphasize the non-Olympian and, therefore,
chthonic character of Plouton. Euboulos, 'the Good Counselor' is a euphemistic title. The story of how he ab-
ducted Persephone (Demeter's daughter of line 12) is
beautifully told in the *Homeric Hymn to Demeter* (2), where
there is no mention of the 'Attic cave' of line 14.

19 - TO ZEUS THE THUNDERBOLT

Zeus is known to have been worshiped as κεραύνιος,
that is, 'God of the Thunderbolt' and as Ἀστραπαῖος,
'Lightener'. This aspect of the chief sky god must be one
of the oldest. Compare Hesiod's *Theogony* where, with the
aid of his dreaded weapon, Zeus subdued the Titans (664ff)
and the monstrous Typhoeus (820ff). The hymn is a prayer
to Zeus as a storm god and, unlike many hymns in this
collection, it is unusually powerful, almost lurid, in its

description of what to the ancients must have been one of the greatest manifestations of divine power.

20 - TO ASTRAPAIOS ZEUS
(see 19 above)

21 - TO THE CLOUDS
The hymn is hauntingly reminiscent of a portion of the homonymous play by Aristophanes. Lines 3-5 could be compared with some of the ideas in lines 368-407 of that play.

22 - TO THE SEA
In this hymn Tethys is identified with the sea. For her genealogy see Hesiod, *Theogony* 132-36. It is through incestuous union with her brother Okeanos that she gives birth to the Rivers and the three thousand Oceanids (Ibid. 337ff).

23 - TO NEREUS
That Nereus was imagined as a wise "Old Man of the Sea" is obvious from *Iliad* 1.358. He is, it should be remembered, grandfather of Achilles through his daughter Thetis. He himself is son of Pontos, and by the Oceanid Doris father of the fifty Nereids (Hesiod *Theogony* 233ff).

24 - TO THE NEREIDS
The catalog of the Nereids is given by Hesiod in *Theogony* 242ff. The Tritons do not appear in Homeric or Hesiodic poetry, and it is really in postclassical times that literature and art makes use of them. Lines 4-5 seem inspired from sculpture. The significance of lines 10-12 is very obscure. Legend had it that Kalliope, one of the nine Muses, was mother of Orpheus (cf. Pausanias 9.30.3 in Peter Levi's translation and Plato *Republic* 364e). Apollodoros in 1.14 (transl. Keith Aldrich) tells us that "Calliope and Oeagrus (though nominally it was Apollo)

had as sons Linus, whom Heracles slew, and Orpheus..."
It seems then that "mother Kalliope" is so called because
she was mother of Orpheus by Apollon.

25 - TO PROTEUS

Proteus in this hymn is more than a wise "Old Man of
the Sea", who is capable of changing his form and of know-
ing both past and future (See *Odyssey* 4.349ff). His later connections with Egypt may be fanciful elaborations
of the account of Menelaos' encounter with him in the
Odyssey. Proteus seems to have been a primeval sea god,
and the hymnist, seizing on the meaning of his name,
"the First", alludes to his cosmogonic role (lines 1, 2,
9).

26 - TO EARTH

Despite lines 1 and 4, this hymn is really addressed
to earth as mother of all life. For Earth's (Gaia's)
role in theogony and cosmogony see Hesiod, *Theogony* 126ff.
The hymn should be compared with *Homeric Hymn* 30.

27 - TO THE MOTHER OF THE GODS

This hymn reminds us of the one to Rhea (14), who is
also called mother of the gods and whose chariot is drawn
by bull-slaying lions. The Hymn to Rhea, however, has
more similarities with *Homeric Hymn* 14 (*To the Mother of
the Gods*). In our *Orphic Hymn* 27 the Mother of the Gods
is identified both with Rhea (much as in *Iliad* 15.187 and
Hesiod's *Theogony* 453, 625, 634) and with Hestia (for
whom see notes on 87). The Mother of the Gods, Gaia,
Rhea, Kybele, and to some extent Demeter are different
faces of the same goddess. Pindar invokes the (Great)
Mother in *Pythian* 3.78 and in *fr.* 85, and in *fr.* 77 identifies her with Kybele.

28 - TO HERMES

For Maia, daughter of Atlas, cf. Hesiod *Theogony* 938

and *Odyssey* 14.435. Argeiphontes, usually translated into 'Slayer of Argos', is of obscure origin and meaning. The phrase "interpreter of all" (6) is the result of folk etymology which connects Hermes with the verb ἑρμηνεύω, 'to interpret'. By Korykos (8) the poet means the Southern promontory of the Erythraean peninsula (opposite Chios). That Hermes is not Κυλλήνιος even once in this hymn should be attributed to the generally Asiatic character of the collection. For Hermes the trickster, thief, inventor of the lyre, etc. cf. the long *Homeric Hymn to Hermes* (4).

29 - HYMN TO PERSEPHONE

For the birth of Persephone see Hesiod *Theogony* 912-14. The same lines contain the reference to Persephone's abduction by Plouton, a theme which is beautifully elaborated in the *Homeric Hymn to Demeter* (2). The title πραξιδίκη ('exacter of justice') with reference to Persephone (5) is not clear. Pausanias tells us that a group of goddesses called πραξιδίκαι were worshiped at Haliartos (9.33.2). 'Mother of the Furies' in line 6 cannot be said *stricto sensu*. The Furies (in Greek Ἐρινύες or Εὐμενίδες) were born of Gaia (Earth) after she had been impregnated by the blood drops from the mutilated genitals of her husband, Ouranos (Hesiod *Theogony* 176-87). Persephone could be said to be their mother in a metaphoric sense, because she reigned inside the dark earth. The "loud-roaring and many-shaped Eubouleus" of line 8 is surely Dionysos, for the Orphics believed that Dionysos was Persephone's son by incestuous union with her father, Zeus. In line 11 Persephone is identified with the Moon (Selene); in lines 16-17 she becomes Mother Earth.

30 - TO DIONYSOS

In this hymn Dionysos is the son of Zeus and Persephone. On the other hand, the adjective "thrice born" (2) obviously alludes to his two other births, once from

Semele, and after her death, from Zeus' thigh, which acted
as some sort of surrogate womb. In *Homeric Hymns* 1 and 26
it is Semele who is his mother. Bacchos (2) and Eubouleus
(7) are titles of Dionysos. Our hymn alludes to his other
natures chiefly as bull-god and god of the vine. Line 5
refers to the ὠμοφαγία, the eating of raw flesh during
sacramental meals when his worshippers became one with the
god. "Triennial feasts", according to our reckoning,
would mean feasts celebrated in alternate years.

31 - HYMN TO THE KOURETES

These semi-divine mountaineers danced about infant
Zeus and clattered their arms in order to muffle the
sound of his crying. Hesiod's *Theogony* tells the story of
how his mother, Rhea, was sent to Crete, but does not mention the Kouretes (468ff). They are, however, mentioned
in Hesiodic *fr.* 123, and among others Kallimachos relates
the episode (*Hymn to Zeus* 52ff, cf. Apollodoros 1.5).
This short hymn is one of the best Orphic Hymns, and the
existence of a religious fraternity which bore the name
Kouretes at Ephesos lends special significance to the
whole collection (see also Ch. Picard, *Éphèse et Claros*
[1922] 279ff).

32 - TO ATHENA

For the Hesiodic account of Athena's birth by Zeus
see *Theogony* 886ff. According to this account Zeus swallowed his consort Metis ('Wisdom'), who was already carrying Athena in her womb. Having done this for fear that
Metis would also give birth to a son who would overthrow
him, he proceeded to place Metis in his own 'womb'.
Homeric Hymn 28 tells the story of Athena's birth from the
head of Zeus (*Theogony* 924). Line 7 refers to the belief
that Athena helped Perseus slay the terrible monster
Medousa, one of the three *Gorgoi* (Hesiod *Theogony* 270 ff).
For the Phlegraian Giants (6) and Athena's role in slaying them see Apollodoros 1.34-39. The title Τριτογένεια

(13) is of unknown origin and meaning.

33 - TO NIKE

Nike (Victory) is first mentioned in Hesiod *Theogony* 384. Lines 2, 3 can only mean that Nike "frees man of the eagerness for contest" by granting him victory. Considering the fervor with which Greeks treated Nike in both religious cult and art, especially sculpture, this hymn can be unique only for the poet's lack of imagination.

34 - TO APOLLON

Paian (1) is thought to have originally meant 'Healer'. In the *Iliad* the title came to be applied to a hymn appropriate to Apollon (the paean), whether invoked as healer (*Iliad* 1.473) or as a god who has conferred victory in martial combat (*Iliad* 22.391-94). Tityos (1) was punished for assaulting Apollon's mother, Leto (*Odyssey* 11.576-81). According to Apollonios Rhodios, Apollon killed him (1.759 ff), but the story is variously told elsewhere (Pindar *Pythian* 4.90; Apollodoros 1.23). *Phoibos* (1) means 'the Bright One'. Lykoreus (1) is obviously connected with *Lykoreia* on the S. slope of Parnassos, above Delphi (Strabo 9.3.3). 'God to whom one cries *ie'* (2) is the translation for ἰήιος. The base of the word may also be seen in the cult title *iepaieon,* and it may not be different from the base of *ie-tros,* 'physician'. Apollon is a Titan (2) on his mother's side. He is called *Grynean* (4) after the Aeolic city of Gryneion (near Kyme) where a temple and an oracle to him existed. *Sminthian* (4) may mean either 'from the town of *Sminthe'* (in the Troad) or, if derived from σμίνθος, 'mouse', may refer to Apollon as destroyer of mice. For the slaying of the monstrous she-dragon Pytho (4) see *Homeric Hymn to Apollon* 300-310 and 355 ff. *Bacchos* (7) reminds us of the mingling of Apollonian and Dionysiac elements. *Didymeus* (7) refers to Didyma (near Miletos) where there was a famous Apollonian oracle. *Loxias* (7) is obscure, but, if derived

from λοξός, 'oblique,' it may refer to the 'obliqueness'
of Apollon's oracles. For Apollon's birth on Delos and
for the establishment of his oracle at Delphi see *Homeric
Hymn to Apollon 3*. Lines 16-23 present Apollon as the
cosmic musician who harmonizes the seasons. The two poles
correspond to the highest and lowest of the three strings
of the musical scale (the lowest string was the highest in
pitch). In this scheme intensity of heat corresponds with
degree of pitch. High pitch (lowest string) goes with
summer and low pitch (highest string) with winter. Spring
is represented by a movement from the highest to the middle string (lowest to intermediate pitch: lowest to
intermediate heat).

35 - TO LETO

Leto is the daughter of Koios and Phoibe (Hesiod
Theogony 404 ff). For Leto's travail and for Apollon's
birth on Delos see *Homeric Hymn to Apollon 3,* lines 1-
126.

36 - TO ARTEMIS

Much as Apollon, Artemis is Titanic on her mother's
(Leto's) side. In less syncretistic times the epithet
Bacchic (2) would be hardly appropriate to Artemis. In
line 3 Artemis is identified with three other goddesses,
Selene (see *Orphic Hymn* 9), Diktynna, and Eileithyia (see
Orphic Hymn 2). Diktynna is a Cretan mountain goddess
worshipped on Dikte in Eastern Crete. Diktynna (frequent-
ly called Βριτομάρτις) had a temple near Kydonia (hence
the allusion in line 12. Cf. Strabo 10.4.13). *Orthia* (8)
refers to the cult of ῎Αρτεμις ᾽Ορθία at Sparta, a cult
which most likely represented a fusion of the pre-Hellenic
Πότνια θηρῶν ('Mistress of Wild Beasts') with an obscure
Doric goddess. This hymn is very different in spirit from
Homeric Hymn 27. Cf. the more ambitious composition by
Kallimachos (*To Artemis* 3).

37 - TO THE TITANS

For the birth of the Titans see Hesiod *Theogony* 132 ff. Line 4 is a reference to the Orphic belief that man was created from the ashes of the Titans whom Zeus burned with his thunderbolt for having torn to pieces and devoured his son Dionysos. The meaning of the last line is not clear. For the descent of men and even gods from the Titans see *Homeric Hymn to Apollon* 3.334-36.

38 - TO THE KOURETES

In this hymn the Kouretes have altogether lost their connection with Zeus and Crete. They are instead identified with the *Korybantes* (for whom see next hymn), the *Dioskouroi,* and especially with the Samothracian *Kabeiroi,* who had themselves been identified with the *Korybantes* and the *Dioskouroi* by the time the Orphic Hymns were composed. The *Kabeiroi* of Samothrace with whom the Kouretes are here identified were most likely of Phrygian origin and their chief function in classical times was to promote fertility and to protect sailors. See also notes on 31.

39 - TO KORYBAS

The Korybantes were not very distinct from the Kouretes (notice how the Korybas of this hymn is also called Koures). As a group they were armed dancing warriors in the train of Rhea - Kybele, while the Kouretes were usually associated with Zeus. Even to Euripides the two groups are not distinct (cf. *Bacchae* 120 ff). Pausanias, however, says that the Korybantes "are quite a different family from the Kouretes" (8.37.6). The Korybas of this hymn seems to have little connection with the Korybantes. In fact he is a nocturnal demon, vaguely reminiscent of Hekate. Interestingly enough, Psellos in his *Quaenam Sunt Graecorum Opiniones de Daemonibus,* 3 (ed. Migne) says that a Korybas and a Koures were mimic forms of demons who were included in the initiation to the Eleusinian mysteries.

Prima facie, this indicates that the pair Korybas - Koures belonged to that part of Orphic - Dionysiac demonology that became connected with Eleusis, at least in the minds of those who tried to unravel the mysteries.

The mythological allusions of lines 5-8 are obscure.

40 - TO ELEUSINIAN DEMETER

For Demeter's connection with Eleusis see the beautiful *Homeric Hymn to Demeter* 2.

41 - TO MOTHER ANTAIA

The epithet ἀνταία, 'besought with prayers,' elsewhere applied to other divinities, here refers to Demeter. For the goddess' wanderings and visit to Eleusis see *Homeric Hymn to Demeter* 2. The Orphic version of Demeter's visit to Eleusis makes Dysaules king and Baubo queen (Clement of Alexandria *Protreptikos* II 20.1-21.2; O. Kern *Orphicorum Fragmenta* 46-53). On Dysaules see also Pausanias 2.14 ff. Our hymn has Demeter visit the Underworld, with the son of Dysaules as her guide. It was Eubouleus, son of Dysaules and brother of Triptolemos, who saw the abduction of Persephone while he was tending his swine (fr. 52).

42 - TO MISE

It is interesting to note that the hymn concerns itself more with Dionysos and less with Mise. *Iacchos* (4) came to be a cult epithet for Dionysos. Originally, he seems to have been the personification of a mystic cry (cf. Aristophanes *Frogs* 316 and Herodotos 8.65), and also, to have been variously thought of as the son of Demeter or Persephone by Dionysos. In this hymn he is the infant Dionysos, an integral part of the motif of divine mother and child. Orphic fragment 52 (Kern) makes him the child of Dysaules and Baubo. Another tradition preserved by Asklepiades of Tragilos (fourth century B.C.) makes Mise

a daughter of the same couple. It is, therefore, probable
that the poet of this hymn was aware of both traditions
and that he addressed Iacchos and Mise together as brother
and sister. The bisexual Mise was Phrygian in origin, and
in the poet's mind she may not have been too different
from the Phrygian Mother of line 6. Note, too, that when
the poet calls Dionysos - Iacchos the "seed of Eubouleus"
he may have in mind not so much Hades as some similar
chthonic deity of the Orphic pantheon (cf. Kern *Orph.*
Frag. 32 c-e).

43 - TO THE HORAI

The names given to the Horai (Seasons) in this hymn
are the same as in Hesiod *Theogony* 902, and they mean
'Law-Abiding', 'Justice', and 'Peace'. In Hesiod they
collaborate with the Graces to deck out Pandora (*Works and*
Days 69-82). They play a similar role in *Homeric Hymn* 6
(*To Aphrodite*). Their number mirrors the idea that the
year is divided into three seasons, winter, spring and
summer.

44 - TO SEMELE

Semele (otherwise called Thyone) is the mother of
Dionysos by Zeus. She was consumed by the fire of Zeus'
thunderbolt when, deceived by the jealous Hera, she asked
her divine lover to appear in his full splendor (cf.
Euripides *Bacchae* 6 ff, Ovid *Metamorphoses* 3.259 ff,
Hyginus *Fabulae* 167, 179). More traditional Orphic belief
held that Persephone was the mother of Dionysos. Pausanias preserves the tradition that Dionysos descended to
Hades and brought his mother back (2.37.5) and in *Olympian*
2.25 ff. Pindar tells us:
> "Long-haired Semele, killed by the roaring thunder-
> bolt,
> now lives among the Olympians,
> beloved of Pallas and Zeus the father,
> and even more beloved of her ivy-bearing son."

45 - HYMN TO DIONYSOS

The epithet βασσαρεύς is derived from the Thracian word βάσσαρα, 'fox', and by extension the 'fox skin' worn in certain Dionysiac festivals. 'Triennial', according to our reckoning, means celebrated in alternate years.

46 - TO LIKNITES

This hymn is addressed to 'Dionysos of the Cradle' (*liknon*). Such a cult existed from early times at Delphi and involved the 'waking up' of the infant Dionysos. This practice tallied rather poorly with the Orphic belief that Dionysos was torn to pieces by the Titans. On the other hand, the practice was connected with the belief that his 'remains' had been brought to Delphi (Plutarch *de Iside* p. 365A). However, the composer of this hymn may rather have had an Asiatic rite in mind, specifically, a 'waking up' of the infant god in the cradle which was more like a resurrection from the Underworld, a resurrection which heralded the rebirth of nature in the spring. (See also Martin P. Nilsson *Geschichte der griechischen Religion* 1: 580 ff). The Hymn should be compared with *Homeric Hymn* 26.

47 - TO PERIKIONIOS

This is a hymn to Dionysos 'twined round the pillar'. The cult to *Dionysos Perikionios* at Thebes may not be unconnected with a reference in Pausanias who reports that, according to local tradition, when Semele was struck by the thunderbolt a log fell down from heaven and that, subsequently, a certain Polydoros (Semele's brother in some sources) decked it out in bronze and called it *Dionysos Kadmos* (9.12.3). There is evidence from classical art that a pillar bearing the mask of Dionysos and bedecked with ivy was an object of worship (cf. Martin P. Nilsson *Geschichte der griechischen Religion*, 1: 207 ff, especially plate 37.1). The first two lines hint at the growth

of ivy, and line 5 seems to refer to a shackled Dionysos
whose shackles come loose. The reader should compare
these lines with lines 16 and 40 of *Homeric Hymn* 7.
Still, the ultimate origins of the cult of *Dionysos Peri-*
kionios remain obscure.

48 - TO SABAZIOS

Here, Sabazios, originally a Thraco-Phrygian deity,
is definitely identified with Zeus. It is interesting to
note that in art he frequently appeared with the thunderbolt and eagle of Zeus. Although private associations
worshiped Sabazios in mainland Greece, Lydia and Phrygia
remained his chief centers of worship. His cult at Pergamum received the strong support of the Attalids.

49 - TO HIPTA

Hipta was a widely worshiped Asiatic mother goddess,
connected especially with Phrygia and Lydia. In this hymn
she is both a nurse of Bacchos and a reveler in the mystic
rites for Sabazios (Sabos), who is frequently identified
with Dionysos.

50 - TO LYSIOS-LENAIOS

Λύσιος means 'he that frees' or 'he that sets loose.'
Although Dionysos as god of wine frees one from cares, it
is entirely possible that the epithet may also refer to
one of those episodes in which the god was bound but freed
himself from his bonds (cf. notes to 47). However, the
epithet Ληναῖος, 'of the wine-press' and the sentiment expressed in lines 5 and 6 point more in the direction of
the soothing side of Dionysos as wine god. Dionysos' two
mothers (1) are Semele and Persephone. The epithet
Ἐπάφιος in line 6 (perhaps also in 52.9) is obscure. It
may be suggestive of the idea that Dionysiac frenzy is a
result of being touched, as it were, by the god.

51 - TO THE NYMPHS

Usually the nymphs are thought of as daughters of
Zeus, but the daughters of Okeanos are nymphs of the sea.
For Pan's association with the nymphs see *Homeric Hymn to
Pan* 19.19 ff. The Hamadryads (14) are nymphs whose life
is coextensive with that of the tree in which they dwell.
The nymphs are linked with Bacchos and Deo (Demeter) in
line 15 because they have power—usually benevolent—over
the places they inhabit. They often acted as nurses of
divine or semidivine children (cf. *Homeric Hymn to Aphrodite* 5.256 ff). The cult of the nymphs in the Greek world
is very old (cf. *Odyssey* 13.356; 17.205 ff).

52 - TO THE GOD OF TRIENNIAL FEASTS

Triennial feasts would be feasts celebrated in alternate years (cf. *Homeric Hymn to Dionysos* 1.11 ff). Zeus
"sewed" the infant Dionysos into his thigh which he used
as a surrogate womb after he rescued him from the burned
body of his mother (cf. Apollodoros 3.26 - 29, Euripides
Bacchae 519 - 27). For Eubouleus (4), usually a title of
Hades, see Hymns 18, 30 and 41. It is not entirely clear
what is meant by "Threefold is your nature..." (5). In
Hymn 30 an epithet which means 'thrice born' is applied to
Dionysos and it implies that he was born of Semele, Persephone, and of the thigh of Zeus. Perhaps his three natures corresponded to his three different 'mothers'. On
the other hand, since Dionysos was devoured by the Titans
and thereby had contact with them, it is possible that his
nature is threefold; human through Semele, Titanic through
the Titans, Olympian through Zeus. And, still, other pos-
sibilities exist, god of frenzy, god of the vine, etc.
In the *Orphica* of the Neoplatonists the epithet 'Erikepaios' (6) is applied to Phanes. This epithet remains
obscure (but see W.K.C. Guthrie *Orpheus and Greek Religion*
97 ff). In line 9 the two mothers are Semele and Persephone. Line 11 identifies Dionysos with Apollon (cf.
Apollon of the golden sword in *Homeric Hymn to Apollon*

3.123, also in *Iliad* 5.509). For *Bassaros* (12) see Hymn
45. See also notes on Hymns 30, 37, 44, 45, 46, 47, 48,
50.

53 - TO THE GOD OF ANNUAL FEASTS

In this hymn Dionysos is Pan, Adonis and Bacchos, and
perhaps even Plouton, all in one. He is the spirit that
wakes nature up and gives the fruit. See also notes on
the preceding Hymn.

54 - TO SILENOS, SATYROS, AND THE BACCHAI

Clearly Silenos, Satyros, the Bacchai, and even the
Naiads are here thought of as followers of Dionysos. Although originally Silenos was more equine in appearance
and Satyros more hircine, eventually the distinction became blurred in the minds of ordinary men, and the Silenoi
were usually imagined as older and wiser satyrs. In fact
Papposilenos (Granddaddy Silenos!), despite his many
weaknesses, was noted for his earthy wisdom. Originally
both Silenoi and Satyrs were naughty, semihuman creatures
of the woodlands, who were eventually linked with Dionysos. The worship of the Naiads (river nymphs or spring
nymphs) must have been very old (cf. *Odyssey* 13.104).

55 - TO APHRODITE

For Aphrodite's birth see Hesiod *Theogony* 190-206.
In this passage Hesiod tells us that the goddess presides
over "maidenly whispers and smiles and tricks, and over
sweet delight and honey-like love" (205-6). Here, however, much as in the *Homeric Hymn To Aphrodite* 5 and in
Lucretius *De Rerum Natura* 1-49, she is not merely the goddess of erotic charm but "giver of birth and of life"
(12). Her dominion over god, man and beast is inescapable.
It is for this reason that she is the "scheming mother of
Necessity" (3). According to the above-mentioned Homeric
Hymn only Athena, Artemis and Hestia are not subject to

her powers of seduction, powers which Zeus himself found
irresistible. The Erotes of line 8 are definitely more
like the winged, playful *putti* of Hellenistic and Roman
art. The concept of Aphrodite riding a swan-drawn chariot
is more proper to Roman poetry. Interestingly enough, in
Sappho 1.10 the chariot of the goddess is drawn by
sparrows.

56 - TO ADONIS

Adonis is an old near Eastern divinity of vegetation
and fertility. The Semitic 'Adon', 'Lord', may reflect
the original meaning of his name. His worship seems to
have come first to Cyprus and from there to have spread
to Greece. Therefore, not only his nature but also his
earlier sojourn in Cyprus explain his special connection
with Aphrodite. Our Hymn makes him offshoot of Aphrodite
and Eros and child of Persephone (8.,9). According to
Apollodoros, Panyasis believed that Adonis was the son of
the Assyrian King Theias by incestuous union with his
daughter Smyrna. Aphrodite who seems to have fallen in
love with the infant Adonis took him to Persephone for
protection, but Persephone herself fell in love with him
and refused to return him. Zeus decreed that Adonis
should spend one third of the year with Persephone, one
third by himself, and one third with Aphrodite. Later on
Adonis was killed by a boar (Apollodoros 3.183-85. For a
different account see Ovid *Metamorphoses* 10.298-559 and
708-39). Aphrodite's love for Adonis reached superb
poetic expression in the *Lament for Adonis,* which since
the renaissance has been attributed to Bion (see
especially lines 43-49).

57 - TO CHTHONIC HERMES

One has the feeling that this Hymn should have been
titled *To Hermes Psychopompos* (Guide of Souls). The claim
that Hermes is the son of Dionysos and Aphrodite does not
agree with the far more traditional belief that he is the

son of Zeus and Maia. Cf. the major *Homeric Hymn to
Hermes 4.*

58 - TO EROS

Despite line 2 which superficially connects Eros
with the winged and cherubic child of Hellenistic and
Roman art, the god of this Hymn is an all-powerful love
god, a veritable match for Aphrodite whom, according to
Hesiod, he follows (*Theogony* 201). In fact he is more
like the primeval Hesiodic god Eros who is younger than
Chaos but coeval with Gaia (Earth). For the irresistibi-
lity of his power see *Theogony* 120-23. In Orphic cosmo-
gonies he seems to have sprung from the primeval egg that
Night laid in the bosom of Erebos (Darkness) and to have
mingled with Chaos, thereby becoming father even of the
gods (Aristophanes *Birds* 693 ff.).

59 - TO THE FATES

The poet alternates between an almost abstract
concept of Fate and the Fates, the three personified
sisters whom he mentions in line 16. (cf. also Hesiod
Theogony 901 ff.). Μοῖρα (and similarly αἶσα) originally
was a man's 'lot' or, more accurately, his alloted 'portion' of life. But a portion conceived as a piece of
yarn (life) has a beginning (birth), and an end (death).
Hence the trebling of what must have been one figure.
Lachesis assigns the lot, Klotho spins the yarn of life,
and the irreversible Atropos cuts it. In Hesiod the Fates
are children of Themis by Zeus and sisters of the Horai
(*ibid.*).

60 - TO THE GRACES

The Hymn follows the Hesiodic account (*Theogony* 907-
11). In the *Homeric Hymn to Aphrodite* 5.60-64 the Graces
are attendants of Aphrodite. In the *Iliad* Diomedes
pierces Aphrodite's robe, which was the handiwork of the

Graces (5.334-39). For the special connection between
Aphrodite and the Graces see Pausanias 6.24.7. They are
frequently connected and even confused with the Horai
(Seasons), and in Hesiod's *Works and Days* (59 ff.)
Aphrodite arms Pandora with πόθος (erotic desire) while
the Graces and the Horai deck her out with seductive
jewels and flowers.

61 - TO NEMESIS

In Homer *nemesis* is a word for 'righteous indigna-
tion,' 'censure,' 'reproach,' etc. In Hesiod the concept
is developed into a personified sinister force, Nemesis,
who is the daughter of Night and Okeanos (*Theogony* 223).
In this poem Nemesis does not seem to be especially harsh
and sinister, or for that matter very different from Dike.
Pausanias, who reports on her sanctuary at Ramnous and on
a famous statue of her carved by none other than Pheidias,
calls her "the especially implacable goddess to evil and
violent men" (1.33.2-4, cf. also 7.20.5). According to
a rather odd myth reported by Apollodoros, Nemesis was the
real mother of Helen: Zeus pursued Nemesis who changed
into a goose, and taking the form of a swan he had inter-
course with her. The goose that was in reality Nemesis
laid an egg which was brought to Leda. The egg hatched
out and Helen was born of it and subsequently reared as
Leda's own daughter (3.127). The poet of our hymn
ignores this sort of mythological lore and concentrates
on Nemesis as a personified abstraction.

62 - TO DIKE

Dike is not really different from Justice in the
next Hymn. Much as νέμεσις, δίκη (custom, law, justice,
etc.) in Homer is not personified. For Hesiod she is
Dike, the daughter of Zeus and Thetis and the sister of
Eunomie (Law-Abiding) and Eirene (Peace). For the account
of her birth see *Theogony* 900 ff. (cf. Hesiod *Works and
Days* 213 ff.). For the concept of Dike sharing the throne

of Zeus cf. Hesiod *Works and Days* 256 ff. and Sophocles
Oedipus Coloneus 1382. Orphic Theologians and Neoplatonists elevated Dike to a position of great importance.
In a speech attributed to Demosthenes we are told that,
according to Orpheus, Dike sat by the throne of Zeus and
watched over all the affairs of mortals (Kern, *Orphicorum
Fragmenta* 23).

63 - TO JUSTICE

Dikaiosyne, 'Justice' is a later personification,
and as such, unlike Dike, has no mythological lore
attached to her. For the rest, cf. Hymn 62.

64 - HYMN TO NOMOS

Nomos, 'Law', in this Hymn is more than 'law' in the
ordinary sense of the word. He represents a cosmic
principle which sees to it that both the inanimate
elements of nature and the creatures that live in them
keep to their proper limits. Nomos is not personified
in Hesiod who uses the word in the sense of 'custom',
'usage' (*Theogony* 66) and 'law' (*Works and Days* 276, cf.
also *Theogony* 417). An early tendency to personify *nomos*
can be seen in the famous Pindaric *Fragment* 152 ("*nomos*
is lord of all") and in Euripides *Hecuba* 800 (cf. also
Orphicorum Fragmenta 105, 160).

65 - TO ARES

Cf. *Homeric Hymn to Ares* 8. In the present Hymn
Ares is asked to change his martial character and to
yield to the charms of Kypris (Aphrodite) and to the
ecstasy which can be found in the revels of Lyaios. Deo
of line 8 is another name for Demeter, and the warlike
god is asked once again to trade spear for sickle.

66 - TO HEPHAISTOS

In the *Homeric Hymn to Hephaistos* 20 Hephaistos

is hymned as a teacher of fine crafts and skills to man
whom he thereby elevated from savagery to civilization.
In the present Hymn Hephaistos is fire as a cosmic element
and fire as the animating or rational principle in the
body. Even as early as in the times of Homer the god's
name became synonymous with fire (e.g. *Iliad* 2.426). It
is entirely possible that the Hymn has Stoic affinities.
The Stoics taught that of all the elements fire is closer
to the nature of the λόγος and that fire periodically
destroys the world so that the creative process may start
anew. Lines 6, 7 are hauntingly reminiscent of ideas
attributed to Heraclitus (cf. Fragments 30, 31, 90 in
Diels-Kranz: 220, 221, 222 in Kirk-Raven). In Athens
Hephaistos and Athena were worshipped together as patrons
of arts and crafts (cf. Plato *Kritias* 109c, 112b; *Laws*
920d; *Protagoras* 321d). For their place in Orphic belief
see Kern, *Orphicorum Fragmenta* 178, 179.

67 - TO ASKLEPIOS

It seems that originally Asklepios was a hero-
physician who was raised to divine status. In the *Iliad*
he is called a "blameless physician" (11.518). For the
story of his birth see Hesiod *Fragment* 58; Pindar *Pythian*
3; Ovid *Metamorphoses* 2.600-34. See also *Homeric Hymn to
Asklepios* 16.

68 - TO HYGEIA

Hygeia (usually spelled Hygieia) is said to be a
daughter of Asklepios, the deified physician (in the
preceding Hymn, line 7, she is his consort). She is
'Health' personified and worshipped as a goddess (cf.
Pausanias 2.11.6). In the Hippocratic oath her name
follows that of Asklepios, and one wonders whether this
sequence is mirrored in the arrangement of the two Orphic
Hymns devoted to them.

69 - TO THE ERINYES

The Erinyes (Furies) were born of the Earth (Gaia)
after she was fertilized by the blooddrops from the
severed genitals of Ouranos (*Theogony* 175 ff.; cf. *Iliad*
19.259). They are malevolent spirits of retribution for
murder, especially murder within the family or clan.
However, there was an early feeling that even natural
phenomena fell within their sphere of power (cf. the
dictum of Heraclitus that the Erinyes would find even the
Sun if he left his course: 94 Diels-Kranz). In this Hymn
they are conceived of as infernal female divinities who
have the power to confer benefits. Apollodoros gives the
same names for the Erinyes (1.3) and reports that bizarre
story that Adrastos' horse Areion was born of Demeter
after she assumed the likeness of an Erinys to have inter-
course with Poseidon (3.77). In origin the Erinyes were
either the ghosts of slain persons or personifications of
curses that called for revenge.

70 - TO THE EUMENIDES

The word Εὐμενίδες, 'The Gracious Ones', seems to
have originally been a euphemistic or propitiatory name
for the Erinyes. That they are not really different from
the Erinyes is obvious to all who have read the *Eumenides*
of Aeschylus. The euphemistic and propitiatory nature of
the epithet Eumenides is plain from such lines as Sophocles *Oedipus Coloneus* 486 and Euripides *Orestes* 38. The
fact that lines 2-3 of the Hymn refer to them as daughters
of Chthonic Zeus and Persephone is no more than another
way of saying that they are truly Stygian and infernal.

71 - TO MELINOE

Unless there has been textual corruption, the story
alluded to in this hymn is quite peculiar, and the details
are wholly obscure. In fact, this hymn is the only
literary testimony to the existence of Melinoe. The name

has turned up in an inscription as an epithet of Hekate
(see W.C.K. Guthrie, *Orpheus and Greek Religion*, 259), a
fact which when coupled with the evidence from this hymn,
supports the suspicion that Melinoe was some sort of
infernal female demon, perhaps yet another persona of
Hekate.

72 - TO TYCHE

Tyche, 'Fortune' or 'Lot', is the personification of
a concept that became very prominent in Hellenistic and
especially in Roman times when she was fully identified
with Fortuna. She is not found in Homer but for Hesiod
she is one of the Okeanidai (*Theogony* 360). In the
Homeric Hymn to Demeter 2 she is among Persephone's companions (420). The tendency toward making Tyche into an
abstraction is quite early. For Alcman she is the
daughter of Forethought and the sister of Law-Abiding and
Persuasion (Page *PMG fr.* 64 - Bergk 62, Diehl 44). In
the beginning of *Olympian* 12 Pindar invokes her as 'Tyche
the Savior'. The word occurs frequently in the tragedians
but it is rarely personified (cf. Sophocles *Oedipus
Tyrannus* 977 and 1080; Euripides *Hecuba* 786). The concept, even in its personified aspect, has been tenacious
and one that still survives in Greece. For obvious
reasons there has been some confusion with Moira (Fate).
In myth and cult she plays a negligible role. The present hymn to some extent identifies her with Hekate.

73 - TO THE DAIMON

This is an invocation to Zeus Ploutodotes, 'Zeus the
Giver of Wealth'·. In the *Homeric Hymn to Demeter* 2 we
are told that it is Demeter and Persephone who send
Ploutos 'Wealth', to those whom they favor (486-89), and
in the *Homeric Hymn to Earth Mother of All* 30 it is
Mother Earth that bestows wealth upon her favorites (7-
12). In *Orphic Hymn* 40.3 Demeter is described as

πλουτοδότειρα, 'giver of wealth', and in the *Thesmophor-iazousai* of Aristophanes (296) Ploutos is invoked in prayer after Demeter and Persephone. The connection of Ploutos with Plouton (Hades) is paralleled in cult and myth by the special relations of Demeter-Kore with the lord of the Underworld. The idea behind this connection may be that Demeter and Kore (Persephone) cannot grant the riches that the earth bears without the collaboration of the god who rules what exists beneath its surface. It is entirely possible that it is because Hades/Plouton, to whom πλουτοδότης would be more proper, is occasionally called Zeus that Zeus himself may eventually come to be addressed as 'giver of wealth'. πλουτοδότης applied to Zeus is a late development in Asia Minor. Pausanias reports that Ζεὺς πλούσιος, 'Zeus of Wealth', had a temple in Sparta (3.19.7). The general tenor of the present Hymn leads me to believe that the poet is not addressing the Olympian Zeus.

74 - TO LEUKOTHEA

For Leukothea see note on *Orpheus to Mousaios* 35 (cf. also Apollodoros 1.80 ff., 84; also 3.26-29). Pausanias reports that in Laconian Brasiai the inhabitants claimed that the wandering Ino arrived at Brasiai and wanted to be Dionysos' nurse. They also showed him the grotto where she brought up the infant Dionysos (3.24.4).

75 - TO PALAIMON

In this Hymn Palaimon is a benevolent sea god. In myth he is Ino's son Melikertes who was transformed into the sea god Palaimon, much as Ino became the sea goddess Leukothea. See notes on preceding Hymn and on *Orpheus to Mousaios* 35.

76 - TO THE MUSES

Cf. Hesiod's *Theogony* 1-103. The Muses are the

daughters of Zeus and Mnemosyne (*Theogony* 53 ff.). The
list given in this Hymn follows the same order as the
Hesiodic *Theogony* 77-79. In the Homeric tradition they
are graceful and benevolent deities who inspire artists
and especially poets and who frequently sing as Apollon
plays the lyre (*Iliad* 1.601-4; *Homeric Hymn to Apollon*
3.189-93 and *to Hermes* 4.450-52). From very early times
the Muses became personifications of man's loftiest
creative aspirations. Their distinction according to
field of creative endeavor is late. 'Agne, the Pure One',
in line 10, seems to be used as an epithet of Mnemosyne.
Cults of the Muses existed in numerous places in Greece.
It will be remembered that in the *Republic* 364 (Book 2)
Plato takes to task certain itinerant charlatans who
claim that Mousaios and Orpheus were the offspring of the
Muses.

77 - TO MNEMOSYNE

The poet is highly conscious of the fact that
Mnemosyne means 'Memory'. It is quite possible that the
goddess of *Iliad* 1 and the Muse of *Odyssey* is none other
than Mnemosyne herself. It is interesting that when
Hermes sings to his lyre he first pays tribute to
Mnemosyne (*Homeric Hymn to Hermes* 4.429 ff.).

78 - TO DAWN

Dawn ('Ήώς) is the lovely goddess on whom Homer
lavishes some of his most beautiful epithets (e.g. 'rosy-
fingered', 'saffron-cloaked'). She is the daughter of
Hyperion and Theia and the sister of the Sun and the Moon
(Hesiod *Theogony* 371 ff.). Many of her lovers came to an
unhappy end (So Orion in *Odyssey* 5.121 ff., cf. also
Apollodoros 1.27). In Homer she is the consort of
Tithonos (*Odyssey* 5.1), whose tragic story is recounted
in the *Homeric Hymn to Aphrodite* 5.218 ff.

79 - TO THEMIS

In this Hymn Themis, in addition to being a Titaness
and a daughter of Ouranos and Gaia (Sky and Earth; for
this see Hesiod *Theogony* 116 ff. and especially line 135),
is a manic prophetess, a sort of primeval Pythia who
taught Apollon the art of giving laws. It is interesting
that according to Aeschylus (*Eumenides* 1-7) Gaia, the
first prophetess at Delphi, was succeeded by her daughter
Themis, and she in turn by Phoibe. In Aeschylus' *Prome-*
theus Bound we are told not only that Themis through
prophecy warned her son Prometheus, but, more importantly,
that she and Gaia are one figure called by many names
(209-25). The revered position of Themis as a prophetess
is also clear from Pindar's *Isthmian* 8.34 ff. The name
Themis means 'established custom or law.'

80 - TO BOREAS

Boreas is the north wind.

81 - TO ZEPHYROS

Zephyros, originally any westerly wind, came to be
thought of as the West Wind proper.

82 - TO NOTOS

Notos is the south wind, and as such opposite to
Boreas.

83 - TO OKEANOS

This hymn reflects standard Homeric belief. According to Homer Okeanos is a mighty river which encircles
the Earth and from which all life, including the gods,
came (cf. *Iliad* 14.201, 246, 302). Significantly, when
Hephaistos makes the wondrous shield of Achilles he
represents Okeanos on its rim (*Iliad* 18.607). In the
Hesiodic *Theogony* he is the son of Gaia and Ouranos (133)

and the husband of his sister Tethys by whom he begets
the rivers and the three thousand Okeaninai ('daughters
of Okeanos;' see *Theogony* 337 ff.).

84 - TO HESTIA

Hestia, the virgin goddess of the hearth, was the
first child born to Rhea and Kronos. Because she was the
oldest child she was the first to be swallowed by Kronos
and the last to be disgorged (Hesiod *Theogony* 454 and
495 ff.). Her Roman counterpart, the hearth goddess
Vesta, was also a virgin goddess worshipped by priestesses
who had to remain chaste during their service to the
temple. Line 2 is paralleled by line 30 in the *Homeric
Hymn to Aphrodite* 5. The same Hymn tells us that Hestia
is one of the three goddesses who are not deceived by
Aphrodite; the other two are Artemis and Athena (7 ff.).
Much of the domestic piety was lavished on Hestia, and
she was the first and the last deity to whom libations
were poured at a public feast. But she was also a civic
deity, since public buildings included a hearth to which
much sacral importance was attached. She was frequently
invoked together with Zeus, and in time the two deities
merged in the concept of *Zeus Ephestios*, 'Zeus of the
Hearth' (for the beginnings of such a concept cf.
Odyssey 14.158-9). The phrase 'you dwell in the house
center' (2) must have originated in the plan of the
Homeric *megaron* which had its hearth in the center. Cf.
also the two *Homeric Hymns* to her, numbers 24 and 29.

85 - TO SLEEP

Quite appropriately, Ὕπνος, 'Sleep,' is said to be
a brother of Λήθη (Oblivion) and Θάνατος (Death).
According to the Hesiodic *Theogony* Death and Sleep are
children of Night (211-12; 758-59), but Oblivion (Λήθη)
was born of Ἔρις (Strife: 226-27). In the Homeric
epic, too, he is the personified brother of Death and

Hera enlists his services in order to put Zeus to sleep
(*Iliad* 14.224 ff.; cf. *Iliad* 16.681-82 where Sleep and
Death carry Sarpedon's body to Lykia). Incidentally, the
first line of the Hymn may be a direct echo of *Iliad*
14.233 in which Sleep is called "Lord of all gods and of
all men." The beginning of book 24 of the *Iliad* is a
beautiful illustration - the oldest description of the
torments of insomnia - of what happens to those whom this
"all-taming lord" does not visit. Cf. also the lively
choral invocation to Sleep in Sophocles *Philoctetes*
827 ff.

86 - TO DREAM

Dream ("Ονειρος) already personified in the *Iliad*
(2.6, 8, 16, etc.) is also a child of Night and a brother
of Sleep and Death (*Theogony* 212, where Hesiod speaks
of 'the race of Dreams'). In as much as interpretation
of dreams must be one of the oldest forms of divination,
lines 2, 6 are quite appropriate. For the prophetic
significance of dreams the reader should turn to the
Oneirokritikos of Artemidorus.

87 - TO DEATH

The personification of Θάνατος (Death) is rather
weak in this poem. It will be remembered that in the
Alcestis of Euripides Herakles wrestles with Thanatos in
order to rescue Alcestis. In the same tragedy he is
strongly personified and called "dark-cloaked lord of the
dead" (843). In the *Frogs* Aristophanes has Aeschylus say
"of the gods Thanatos alone loves no gifts" (1392). The
phrase "common to all" of line six seems to echo the
Homeric epithet ὁμοίιος, 'leveling,' which death - not
necessarily personified - shares with such banes as war
and old age (cf. *Odyssey* 3.236; *Iliad* 4.315; 9.440 etc.).
Lines 3, 4 reflect a definitely Orphic belief (for which
see Introduction). For obvious reasons Thanatos and

Charon, sometimes confused even in antiquity, have
totally merged in the Modern Greek figure of Charos with
whom Digenes and other epic figures wrestle in "the
marble threshing floors" of folk poetry. See also notes
on 85 and 86.

SELECT BIBLIOGRAPHY

Reference Works

The Oxford Classical Dictionary (Oxford : Clarendon
    Press, [2]1970)
Der Kleine Pauly, 5 volumes (Stuttgart & München :
    Druckenmüller, 1964-75)
Ausführliches Lexikon der griechischen und römischen
    Mythologie, edited by Wilhelm Heinrich Roscher.
    7 volumes (Leipzig : Teubner, 1884-93)

Editions

Eugen Abel, *Orphica*. Accedunt Procli Hymni, Hymni Magici,
    Hymnus in Isim, aliaque eiusmodi carmina (Lipsiae &
    Pragae : Freytag & Tempsky, 1885)
Wilhelm Quandt, *Orphei Hymni* (Berlin : Weidmann, 1955;
    [2]1962)

Secondary Literature

For an extensive bibliography on the Hymns, see Quandt,
    2nd edition, 58-61, 90.
Felix Graf, *Eleusis und die orphische Dichtung Athens in
    vorhellenistischer Zeit,* Religionsgeschichtliche
    Versuche und Vorarbeiten 33 (Berlin : de Gruyter,
    1974)
William K.C. Guthrie, *Orpheus and Greek Religion* (London :
    Methuen, 1935)
Idem, *The Greeks and Their Gods* (Boston : Beacon Press,
    [2]1954)
Otto Kern, "Das Demeterheiligtum von Pergamon und die
    orphischen Hymnen," Hermes 46 (1911) : 431-36
Idem, "Mysterien," PRE 16/2 (1935) : 1283-85
Rudolf Keydell, "Orphische Dichtung, I) Hymnen," PRE
    18/2 (1942) : 1321-33
Ivan M. Linforth, *The Arts of Orpheus* (Berkeley & Los
    Angeles : University of California Press, 1941)
Christian August Lobeck, *Aglaophamus; sive de theologiae
    mysticae Graecorum causis* (Regimontii Prussorum :

55845

Bornträger, 1829)

Ernst Maass, *Orpheus. Untersuchungen zur griechischen,
römischen, altchristlichen Jenseitsdichtung*
(München : Beck, 1895)

Martin P. Nilsson, *Geschichte der griechischen Religion,*
vol. I^3, II^2 (München : Beck, 1967; 1961)

Ulrich von Wilamowitz-Moellendorff, *Der Glaube der Hel-
lenen,* 2 volumes (Darmstadt : Wissenschaftliche
Buchgesellschaft, ^{3}1959)

Günther Zuntz, *Persephone* (Oxford : Clarendon Press, 1971)

DEMCO